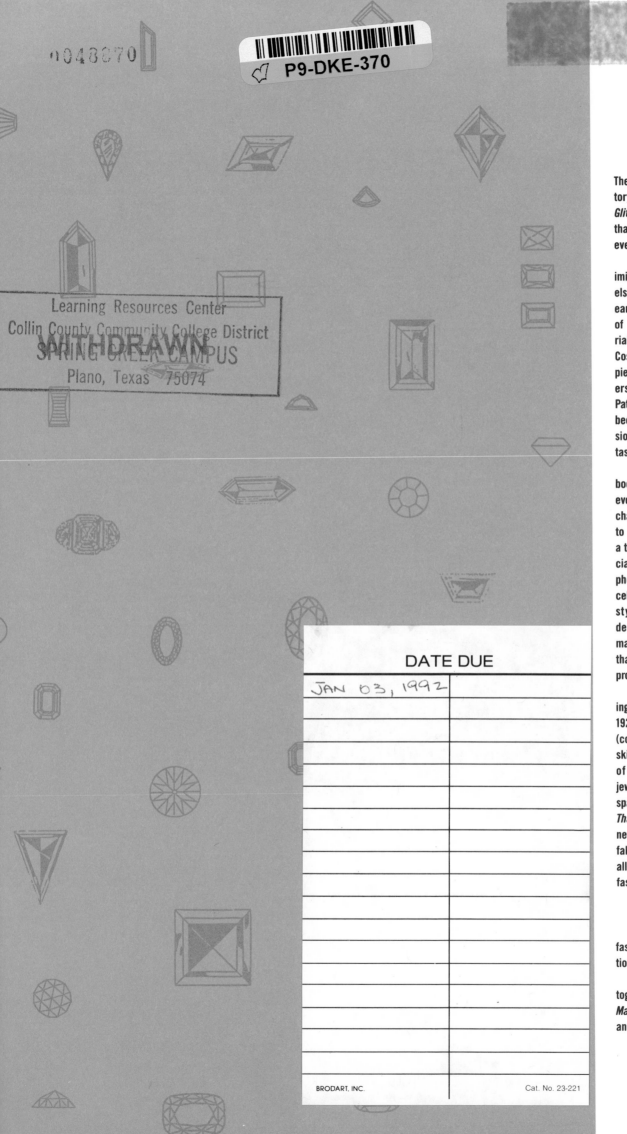

The first glamorous, in-depth history of costume jewelry, *All That Glitters,* explores a form of fashion that is more popular today than ever before.

Originally viewed as a cheap imitation of the real thing, faux jewels came into their own during the early 1920s (when they were made of such obviously "unreal" materials as plastic, wood, and cork). Costume jewels became signature pieces at the hands of such designers as Chanel, Schiaparelli, and Patou, and since their time have been considered an opulent extension, rather than an erosion, of taste.

This luxuriously illustrated book follows its subject as it has evolved to the present day. The six chapters, each of which is devoted to a different decade, incorporate a treasure-box of vintage and specially commissioned contemporary photographs (including those of celebrity jewelry wearers who set style in movies, fashion, and design), period advertisements, magazine covers, and illustrations that have never before been reproduced.

A lively, irreverent text featuring anecdotes and gossip—on the 1920s craze for "suntan pearls" (colored to match the beach goer's skin tone); the Disney cartoon pins of the 1940s, and the "body jewelry" of the 1960s—round out a sparkling parade through time. *All That Glitters* introduces a whole new generation to the fun of the fake and will delight collectors and all observers of fashion and the fashionable.

Jody Shields has written on fashion for a variety of publications, most recently Italian *Vogue.*

Max Vadukul's fashion photography has appeared in *Vogue, Mademoiselle, New York Woman,* and *The New York Times Magazine.*

ALL THAT GLITTERS

Jody Shields

Photographs
Max Vadukul,
Paul Lachenauer,
and others

RIZZOLI
NEW YORK

Page 1: vintage costume jewelry photographed at Norman Crider Antiques in New York City; pages 2-3: witty, enameled musical instrument brooch, signed "Schiaparelli," themed to the designer's 1937 fashion collection; pages 4-5: swinging looks from the 1960s (from left to right): Oriental collar and 3-D earrings (worn as hat brooches), chain pendants, exotic pearl and panther necklaces, oversized rhinestone brooch (used as turban ornament), chandelier earrings, and animal and faux Oriental pendant necklaces. Signed "Cadoro," "Kenneth Jay Lane," "Jacques Libuono," "Marvella," and "Napier"; pages 6-7: a harvest of flower and vegetable jewelry, signed "Chanel." Semi-translucent poured-glass brooches and rings, banded with gold metal, date from the early 1960s.

Th

Glory of Costume Jewelry

To My Parents

First published in the United States of America
in 1987 by
Rizzoli International Publications, Inc.
597 Fifth Avenue, New York, NJ 10017

Library of Congress Cataloging-in-Publication Data

Shields, Jody.
All that glitters.

  Bibliography: p.
  Includes index.
  1. Costume jewelry.   I. Title.
NK4890.C67S55   1987
391'.7'0904   87-45489
ISBN 0-8478-0868-8
ISBN 0-8478-0871-8 (pbk.)

*Designed by Keith Davis
and Philip Zimmerman*

Set in type by Rainsford Type,
Ridgefield, CT
Printed and bound in the U.S.A.

Front cover: artificial pearl collar, choker, hair ornament, and earring representative of the fantastical, one-of-kind pieces commissioned by fashion magazines for special pages in the 1960s. Jewelry designed and made by Jules van Rouge. (Photograph by Max Vadukul); *back cover:* "the Lady of the Brobdingnagian Bangles," Nancy Cunard, photographed by Cecil Beaton, 1929. (Photograph courtesy of Sotheby's, London); *front flap:* brilliantly colored wooden beads from mid-1960s, assembled by hand on flexible wire and twisted into a necklace and spiky earrings. A three-dimensional spiral necklace is worn as a hair ornament. Jewelry designed and made by Jules van Rouge. (Photograph by Max Vadukul); *back flap:* signature 1980s jewelry style—armloads of gold metal charms and bangles, faux watch, and oversized earrings. Jewelry designed by Maripol. (Photograph by Max Vadukul)

The heavenly patron of costume jewelry must be female. Like all good goddesses (and movie heroines), she's blessed with beauty—and a mysterious past. That's apropos for costume jewelry, the fashion item without a history. Why the neglect?

Certainly there is an attitude problem. Chalk it up to the taken-for-granted assumption that costume jewelry is only an imitation of "precious" jewelry. A fake. And because it's made of non-precious materials, it's as if it doesn't deserve a significant look. In truth, costume jewelry does have its own rich history, a history intertwined with fashion. How costume jewelry evolved from a poor copycat to a status symbol and a sensitive register of changing styles, is a twentieth-century story.

Originally, costume jewelry was turned out by "trinket" or "novelty" manufacturers who also made haircombs, handbags, barrettes, and buttons. These jewels mimicked the real thing at a fraction of the cost, and in the better circles the faux didn't go. Costume jewelry, lacking class, was simply—unacceptable.

In the early 1920s costume jewelry came into its glamorous own. A handful of Parisian couturiers began to create costume jewelry to go with their clothing lines, making it not only acceptable, but desirable and expensive. Blessed by high fashion, "junk" materials of no value were transformed into jewelry that was the height of chic. Just one example: a French couturier made a necklace out of cork balls and priced it in America for $30—an astronomical figure at the time. Now that was something to respect! And of course that cork necklace wouldn't have sold unless it was under a fashionable name. Only a few years earlier, the wearing of rhinestones and other fakes was a nearly heinous offense against good taste. With couturier approval, costume jewelry's history also became the history of the reign of the fashion tastemakers.

Massive, sculptural jewelry in simple shapes defined the 1970s. Gold-metal bracelets and necklace (opposite page) finished with a high shine and rough, gravelly textures, signed "Napier."

Over the next six decades, costume jewelry made an endless chain with fashion, woven into a social and emotional meaning of what people wore. And as the definition of style changed to incorporate American outlooks as well as Parisian, new developments in the arts and technology, and especially popular culture and taste, so did jewelry. No fad was immune; costume jewelry picked up the slack where precious gems left off, producing everything from airplane earrings in honor of Charles Lindburgh's flight in the 1920s to hand-grenade charms in the wartime 1940s.

Costume jewelry is uniquely a terrific chronicle of the plurality of fashionable influences that coexisted at any given time. Sometimes that coexistence could be surprising. The 1930s stylish woman took to Victorian-revival jewelry as much as she did to streamlined modern versions; and the "mod" darling of the 1960s went in for heavy Renaissance-style brooches as well as up-to-the minute Lucite earrings. Each decade, however, made a style its own, using its particular experiences and imaginative forces, so that the romance with history in the 1920s and 1930s, say, didn't look the same. Like other fashion ephemera, and perhaps even more so than clothing, twentieth-century costume jewelry can function unaltered only in its own particular time. Once revived, it's revived with a difference. Only in the 1980s has authentic, "antique" costume jewelry (or its look-alikes) become cherished in a new way and mixing actual old and new pieces became fashionable—another change in status for the faux.

As an indication of changing popular sensibility, whimsy is an important clue, and there is a no more reliable record of styles in humor than costume jewelry. With equal aplomb, costume jewelry has embraced the 1920s flapper's exaggerated scads of pearls; the wild giggle of Elsa Schiaparelli's Surrealist-inspired plastic gems in the 1930s; and the soignee humor of the 1950s poodle brooch.

Coco Chanel, instrumental in costume jewelry's history, understood its humor and parody very well. Said she, "When you wear jewels, they should be visible, important, striking . . . wear your real ones at home or among friends, not on the street. You should not wear your fortune around your neck as if you were a savage."

Preceding page: A cascade of gold metal disks, chains, and glass beads make an exotic bib necklace, associated with India in the 1930s; opposite page: quick-drying glue—the jewelry technique of the 1980s—made this rhinestone tiara, necklace, and bracelet possible. Signed "Wendy Gell"; following page: 1940s chandelier earrings, elaborate tiers of tiny glass beads, were assembled by hand. Signed "Miriam Haskell."

CONTENTS

The 1920s prided itself on how quickly everything changed, whether it was clothing, life-style, or consumer goods. "Within our time, the muff has vanished into limbo. The automobile that was a dromedary in 1910 has become a running panther . . . " boasted a 1928 ad. Fashion, that reliable mirror, reflected every dizzying change and created its own upheavals, too. This was the first truly "modern" era, modern in its fast pace, its technology, its designs, and its loosened-up social attitudes—especially women's attitudes. What women wore, how they acted when they wore it, were all modern—and news. Part of what they wore was jewelry—primarily costume jewelry, and lots of it.

In the late nineteenth and early twentieth century, glass beads, fake pearls (copies of the Victorian era's favorite), and a few timid brooches or bracelets still made up costume jewelry's repertoire—definitely second-class. Styles in jewelry (as in fashion and the decorative arts) continued to evolve slowly, and their innovations were reflected in precious gems before reaching their imitation sisters. Costume jewelry had no cachet.

The 1920s changed everything. In the aftermath of World War I, fashion flourished as never before, spurred on by the rise of mass manufacturing, advertising, and popular ladies' magazines, as well as by an unprecedented rise in general income levels and women's new freedoms in behavior and spending.

Fashion began to reflect the new woman, and this baby needed new jewelry. For example, the advent of the female golfer and tennis player was a sign of the times, and women's sportswear was born, the fashion event of the era. The casual, easy-to-wear clothes, in practical fabrics such as jersey or knits, also affected the design of "city" wear, and the sweater-and-skirt ensemble became a new classic. The formality of precious gems didn't suit sportswear. Jewelry of non-precious materials was made to order: there was a freedom in wearing ornaments of no value. Costume jewelry was also contemporary and younger—and youth was the firepower of the 1920s. Couturiers Jean Patou and Coco Chanel were sportswear's advocates; significantly, they were also among the first to offer jewelry that was equally casual.

Three little words describe 1920s high fashion: Paris, Paris, Paris. No original, home-grown American equivalent existed. French couturier clothes and accessories (or their copies) filled the stylish American woman's closet. The creation of costume jewelry was yet another way for the couturiers to stamp their "look" on a client.

Illustration by Tim Sheaffer

Mélange of necklaces (opposite page) made of glass, wood, nuts, seeds, and plastic.

It's difficult to establish which couturier was "first" to create costume jewelry. Paul Poiret is certainly in the running. In the early teens, he accessorized his clothes with necklaces of silk tassels or semi-precious stones designed by the artist Iribe. However, this jewelry was not sold under Poiret's name; apparently it was only for the showroom. One of the first mentions of couturier-"sponsored" jewelry (as it was called) was in 1923, when a French company, Francis Winter & Co., manufactured costume jewelry for couturiers Drécoll, Chanel, and Premet. No one in this list was singled out as the "first" to put his or her name on costume jewelry—they were all successful.

Once the designers stepped in, business boomed. American fashion magazines and store advertisements were full of couturier clothing and the costume jewelry that accompanied it. Fashion's roll call in the 1920s included designers Agnès, Coco Chanel, Madeleine Cherult, Drécoll, Goupy, Jeanne Lanvin, Lucien Lelong, Louiseboulanger, Molyneux, Mary Nowitsky, Jean Patou, Premet, Maggie Rouff, Elsa Schiaparelli, Madeleine Vionnet, and Worth. Even if some of the names were minor talents, all a garment or gem needed was the magic "Paris" on the label.

So great was the demand for couturier "name" designs that in the United States the business of copying the originals also flourished. Fashion texts in magazines, ads, and newspapers blithely billed these goods as a "real Chanel dress copy" or a "Patou pin (copy)." Original couturier jewelry and its knock-offs were advertised side by side. This practice was no shame, as the best stores carried both types of merchandise. While the couturiers weren't happy about the pirating, there was no copyright law to prevent anyone from duplicating dresses or jewelry, or even using the couturier's name to advertise them.

Costume jewelry manufacturers turned out three types of jewelry: bona fide couture originals, their copies, and mass-market baubles. Couture jewelry was imported from Europe, or made in the United States under a licensing agreement with the couturier. The latter was a rare case in the 1920s: only Lanvin, working with the D. Lisner Company, licensed its name. Imported jewelry was the most costly, since the tax imposed on foreign-made goods increased the selling price. Manufacturers could get around the tax by importing jewelry materials and assembling them into finished pieces in the United States. Couturier jewelry was also higher priced due to the famous "name" of its creator and its newness. For top American department stores, the American Napier Company made "private label" couture jewelry; that is, they manufactured it, and the jewelry was sold through the store without a name stamped on it. Unfortunately, very little couturier jewelry—the originals or the copies—were signed. Without an exact sketch or photograph it's impossible to identify a piece of costume jewelry's distinguished lineage.

Couturier jewelry originals and their copies looked nearly identical. But whereas the original may have been plated with real gold or silver and probably came straight from Paris, the copy was most likely made in America, and made more cheaply, with rhinestones glued in, "gems" not set by hand, or using a

Skinny metal bangles (top) worn by the armload. Bracelets in multiples of seven were considered good luck during the 1920s. Costume jewelry from the couturiers of Paris (bottom and opposite page) in the late 1920s.

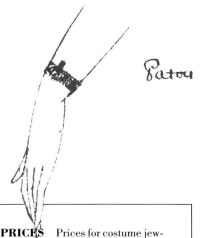

Bracelet of chalcedony, crystal, onyx and chrysoprase.

Patou

PRICES Prices for costume jewelry were wildly disparate. Woolworth's offered costume jewelry for 10 cents an item; the chic Lord and Taylor store sold $60 rhinestone necklaces. In Paris, $100 bought the best-quality, nearly real-looking rhinestone bracelets. (In comparison, $1.89 was the price of a pair of silk stockings.) One month after the 1929 stock market crash, the Bonwit Teller store advertised costume jewelry copies of elaborate real diamond and ruby pieces from Paris. The necklaces of colored rhinestones set in sterling were a staggering $89–$125; bracelets $55–$165; brooches $14–$85. Even post-crash, the wealthy few who could afford frivolity desired rhinestones.

cheaper grade of artificial pearls. Given this situation, it was a measure of a woman's status to wear the couturier original before it was knocked off by the copyists.

On the level below couturier jewelry and its complicated machinations was mass-market jewelry—the kind Filene's store catalog was probably referring to in 1923 when it advised, "The costume rule is: a string of beads for every frock." These were basic items without the rapid style turnover of the top-of-the-line jewelry. This costume jewelry wasn't necessarily cheaper: it could be as expensive and as well made as the couturier pieces, but it did lack the cachet of that famous name. Improved technology also made new types of costume jewelry available more quickly, and in larger quantities. The new manufacturing methods of the plastics industry were a major contribution to costume jewelry's success story. New York City and Providence, Rhode Island were the primary manufacturing centers for these generally lower-priced goods, with their plentiful skilled and cheap immigrant labor forces, From these centers, jewelry was shipped all over the country, sold by traveling salesmen, some working from a horse and buggy. Dime stores, general stores, occasionally even fine jewelers carried a line of costume jewelry. It was also available by mail order from giants such as Montgomery Ward's.

By 1925, costume jewelry was well established, as proclaimed by the Marshall Field's store catalogue, "The imitation is no longer a disgrace." The imitation had been around for some time before it got the nod from an established authority. Not until 1927 did *Vogue*, referring to the craze for suntans and costume jewelry, sigh, "Fashion has decided that all we need ask of an ornament is to adorn us and that neither our complexions nor our gems are to be natural."

This acceptance was symptomatic of an attitude transfusion. "She wears 5 million francs' worth of pearls as if they were not worth a sou," went gossip about Chanel in Paris in 1927. Chanel's offhandedness was translated into a benediction for costume jewelry. Following her lead, women began to flaunt their fake gems for the sake of style, not value.

Most notorious was the flapper. Her looks, mood, make-up, and manners were all carried to excess—and echoed in how she wore her jewels. String-bean skinny, she threw over modesty for short skirts, scissored her long hair into a bob, stayed out until all hours of the morning, and smoked cigarettes (in public)—habits that shocked her "Victorian" parents.

Wholly in keeping with her naughty character, the flapper decked herself out with too much jewelry—and jewelry that was fake, at that. Girls just wanted to be amused. *The Delineator* understood her, pouting, "Most of us count a month lost if it does not bring a new bracelet."

For an evening out on the town, the well-dressed woman might be covered with the entire contents of a big jewelry box: a gem-studded hairband, jeweled pins in the hair, a necklace, rings outside her gloves, long earrings, a brooch, an ornamental clasp at her waist, glittering shoe buckles, and perhaps a fan set with sparkles. Everything but jeweled bells on her toes.

Costume jewelry didn't get an approving embrace from everyone. About those "blazing and jingling gewgaws," Emily Post's 1928 etiquette book sneered, "The woman of uncultivated taste" prefers "wearing bangles to sleeves, rings to gloves." Another etiquette guide from the same date scolded about jewelry, "Do not finger it, nothing is so disagreeable to the on looker than the constant twisting of beads, or swinging them around one's finger, pinning and unpinning one's brooch, or rattling one's rings."

With the exception of the oversized primitive-looking barbaric jewelry that enjoyed a reign of popularity, costume baubles of the 1920s were small in scale. It had to be small jewelry, to work with the clothing, which was generally made of fine, fragile fabrics. The fashionable flat, round, or V-shaped necklines, and lack of dressmaker details made necklaces the ideal accessory. Multiple bracelets were perfectly suited to short sleeves and bare arms. In general, important jewelry pieces were the necklace, earrings, and bracelets. Brooches weren't as standard an accessory as they later became in the 1930s; both hat pins and brooches decorated hats and handbags more frequently than they did lapels.

Inspiration for fashion, and costume jewelry, came from sources as diverse as society gals, Far Eastern influences, current fads, Art Deco and industrial design, and a brand-new source—the movies. Women copied the stars of the silver screen. Notable at this time were a series of peculiar and spectacularly jeweled films (*Sâlomé, Cleopatra, The Ten Commandments, Samson and Delilah*), which promoted the flapper's taste for the exotic. Those lavish movies launched a thousand costumes; masquerade parties were wildly popular, and young, middle-aged, and older women, urban and suburban, dressed themselves like slave girls, Spanish dancers, gypsies, and the maharajah's mistress, complete with outlandish jewels. Costume jewelry was a theatrical accessory, and the distinction between dressing for a costume party and dressing for a restaurant dinner began to blur.

Jeweled women were legion—and legendary. Anna Held, a Ziegfeld Follies star, matched her garters and shoes to her dress, both decorated with costume gems. Stylish eccentric Baba de Faucigny Lucinge pinned bunches of jeweled grapes to her swim suit. Jenny, one of the dancing Dolly sisters, won several million francs gambling in Monte Carlo, which she spent on glass-fronted cases for her home to display a showstopping jewelry collection. Jenny was a truly modern girl—she bought her own jewels.

A Parisian's lavish way with pearls captured by photographer Brassai.

PEARLS The flapper didn't go in for the short, sweet, one-pearl-strand-around-the-neck look. Much more imaginative, she hoisted ropes of pearls around her neck, sometimes a half dozen strands at a time. Pearl necklaces were wound around her neck, her wrist, and her upper arm. Pearls were draped around her shoulders. Pearl necklaces dangled to the flapper's knees, tied in a giant knot at the end.

According to 1920s standards of taste, the perfectly worn pearl necklace should lie completely flat on the body. Unfortunately, a too-ample bosom spoiled that effect for some ladies. Those fortunates, the flat-chested females, rejoiced. Fashion's about-face in the latter part of the decade saw dresses cut way down low in back. That meant that the pearl necklace was worn backward, gleaming against bare skin, which was sometimes exposed all the way to the waist. It was the curvier females who rejoiced this time.

What went down came up again, and the long pearl necklace (or sautoir) lost its cachet, replaced by pearls hiked up into short graduated strands. Two, three, five, or even ten thick rows of pearls were draped around the neck. Tiny seed pearls were also a late 1920s development, most commonly worn as thick short chokers, made from three or more strands braided together.

MODERN STYLE

"We moderns" was the way the Saks Fifth Avenue store advertising addressed customers. That brisk familiarity told the tale of the 1920s attitude—a touch of arrogance, a clubby smugness. The 1920s claimed the modern style as their very own; there was no "modern" before them. Birthed like some mythological goddess, the modern style rose, fully formed, from the sea of art and industry and was greeted with a giddy enthusiasm.

Opened in Paris in 1925, the Exposition Internationale des Arts Décoratifs et Industriels Modernes was the cradle of what came to be known as the Art Deco or Moderne style. In its aftermath, consumer goods from kitchen appliances to furniture, as well as architecture, succumbed to the charms of its stylized geometry. The slang expression of the day was "go modern," used to indicate the style, as well as a measure of the restless, fashionably up-to-date attitude.

Fashion had the "go modern" spell cast on it, too. "The plane, the cone, the cylinder and the sphere of modern art have a powerful influence on modern costume, making what seems to be a really new period," bragged a Marshall Field's store catalog, adding, "perhaps one of equal importance with the Egyptian and the Greek." It just wasn't possible to accessorize a modern dress with a locket or a fancy, old-fashioned brooch; costume jewelry filled the need for a new type of ornament perfectly.

At its most basic definition, the purely modern style of Deco jewelry (since Deco design and jewelry were also influenced by the shapes and colors of the exotic objects displayed at the Paris exposition) was geometric, a glorified echo of machine forms. The fussy, the sentimental, and the representative were rejected; the abstract ruled. Jewelry had a surface texture that was sleek, smooth, and streamlined. Plastic, glass, and metal were favored materials. Certain luxurious materials (ivory and ebony) also made up the modern jewelry vocabulary. Modern jewelry of the 1920s had a characteristically lightweight, two-dimensional appearance. It wasn't jewelry of breathtaking beauty, but it can be appreciated for its clever, appropriate "rightness." Like a piece of machinery, it was faintly anonymous—and that was just the idea.

Geometric shapes were commonly used for jewelry, often because technically it was simply easier to produce rectilinear pieces. A more precise insight is given in the 1983 publication *American Design Ethic:* "The action of instruments and machines was essentially geometric, as were the forms of the materials available for production (sheets, tubes, wires). As a result, it was natural at the time to presume that geometric forms were most suited to machine production and that such qualities as mathematical accuracy and purity of finish would bring pleasure to those seeking manufactured perfection." Fashion had a quirkier definition of the modern impulse: "Simplicity," said couturier Lucien Lelong, "is the cocktail in art."

Black Bakelite necklace (top) is a lanky four inches long. Clear glass beads (opposite page) fancifully worn in rows. In 1925 a single one of these necklaces cost 98 cents.

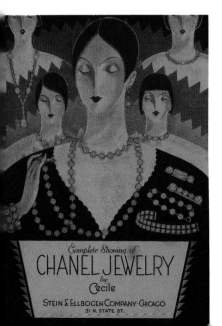

If there had been a prize for the most modern jewelry material, plastic would have won. Plastic was the embodiment of the purest form of the modern spirit: it could be molded into clean, simple shapes, it wasn't precious, and it didn't need ornamentation. The triangular beads, disks, and rectangular slabs had no historical reference—they seemed to be crafted by some otherworldly hand. With its cool assurance, this severe jewelry didn't have a sentimental glitter in its hard little body.

No less than the curator of Industrial Art at the Metropolitan Museum in New York supported the advancement of modern jewelry. He prophesied, "Those who design jewelry today should realize that this is an age of locomotives, of automobiles and typewriters. The making of jewelry is an ancient craft and a noble one, but should it be less progressive than automobile manufacturing? . . . the natural follow-up in jewelry design would be the fashioning of ornaments in some modern substance—in the same way as Bakelite has been used in costume jewelry."

At the tail end of the 1920s, as the rigidity of the geometric loosened up, a new material became the working definition of "modern." That material was transparent, colorless "Prystal," a composition plastic. Prystal had a hygienic, heartless, machine-made elegance. However, the 1920s love of luxury often betrayed the machine Deco style. Prystal jewelry had plain and simple shapes—but it was also gussied up with ornate, hand-carved detailing.

The Deco taste also affected even the more traditional stone-set costume jewelry. Bracelets were nothing more than a row of rhinestones linked together; earrings, a fall of stones. Unnecessary details were eliminated, and eventually even the stone's setting was nearly done away with, or at least made inconspicuous. This was a revolutionary concept. Before that innovation, the setting (the elaborately worked metal surrounding a gem) had always been a jeweler's pride and joy, the demonstration of his skill. Now the stone, held in place with a simple prong, got all the glory.

The new devaluation of the setting was a boon to costume jewelry. It could be copied easily from the precious original models, it was simple to manufacture, and it was very fashionable. Important enough to get the attention of the fashion magazines, modern jewelry was mentioned in *Fashionable Dress*, along with new hairstyles: "New methods of setting jewelry and new methods of setting waves go share and share alike in the illustrious honors of making us more beautiful."

Trendsetting designer Coco Chanel created her own new "minimal" gemstone setting. A thin band of metal was wrapped around the edge of a brilliant-cut stone ("crystal"). Linked together on a necklace, crystals were free of their settings, nearly totally transparent, and open to the play of light. In the spring of 1928 *Women's Wear Daily* referred to these specially set, triangular stones as "nailheads" and "Chanel stones." Chanel used the same setting for her fake and semi-precious colored stones strung with pearls. Another Chanel variation on the simplified, modern theme was a chain set with rhinestones, spaced a few inches apart. With her dry sense of humor, Chanel called this necklace a "river of diamonds." *Fashionable Dress* referred to this spare jewelry in 1927: "Modern, too . . . are the new forms of setting worked out like ring mountings so that the metal is scarcely discernible, the jewels looking as if they stood alone or were just wished together. The effect is emphatically rich."

To look rich but understated was ultra-modern. The *Jeweler's Circular* magazine noted, slightly defensively, "As the memory of the Great War and the profiteer sinks into oblivion, everyone wants to look as if 'they belonged,' and it is by concealing the magnificence of their jewelry that they succeed." Diamond necklaces were ". . . now notable by the manner in which they are mounted, the idea being to use the gems sparsely . . . one touching the other would have an almost too rich appearance, and the ingenuity of the jeweler is being applied to making diamonds look natural and not rich."

A reversal for jewelry, the idea also affected the clothing with which modern gems were worn. Chanel was the top practitioner of the "deluxe poor look," as it was called. Her suits, made of jersey (an ordinary fabric never used in couture), were plain, very expensive, and made the wealthy women who wore them "chic on the edge of poverty." True to form down to the last detail, *Collier's* magazine gossiped that Chanel herself wore luxurious silk lingerie and "permitted not a scrap of lace" to trim it. Rhapsodizing in *Studio* magazine, Aldous Huxley wrote, "Modern simplicities are rich and sumptuous; we are Quakers, whose severely cut clothes are made of damask and cloth of silver. . . ."

Cubistic cut lumps of topaz glass make a necklace (opposite page, top). Another choker (opposite page, bottom) mixes steel beads and pearls. Chanel's 3-D plastic beads (below, right) date from 1929. She was also credited with the glass and metal beads shown above. Tiny rhinestones stud transparent plastic bangles (below).

ROMANTIC REVIVALS

The hard-boiled flapper's hard-edged jewelry—strewn with glittery stones—had its flip side: jewelry with a sentimental aura, a romantic association. Historical periods and personalities from the Rococo to the Victorian fed a revival of fussy baubles that were detailed with twisting garlands, filigree, and looping swags of ribbon and drapery. And Mother's standard—pearls—was put to new uses, becoming the symbol of the 1920s.

Pearls, Pearls, Pearls

"Pearls," sniffed *The Delineator* magazine in 1927, "are so becoming women cannot be turned from them even by their own cooks and parlour maids." Everyone, rich and poor alike, loved pearls, the true and the faux. They were the indispensable accessory—the emblem of the 1920s.

Thanks to the flapper, pearls lost their demureness. Pearls were the single-strand standard of matrons and timid maidens until the flapper made them her own. She wore pearl necklaces by the dozens, wore them for their lustrous flattery and the drama of their shake and sway. While one string of artificial pearls could pass for the real thing, a sultan's ransom of fakes was too much to believe. The flapper put on her pearls with a wink and a smile, knowing they weren't believable—her attitude made pearls modern.

It's curious that pearls, so romantic, were jewelry bait for the flapper in a time when the geometric, the hard, the machine-made were the desired style; pearls, in their own way, did reflect some of these characteristics: uniform perfection, a sublime, non-craftsmanlike appearance, and luxury.

Once upon a time, pearls were for millionaires and royalty only. In the 1920s both millionaires and royalty were put to work as pitchmen (and women) for artificial pearls. Orienta, one of the notable fake-pearl companies, used a genuine titled personality as an example in their ads—Queen Marie of Rumania. Marie's royal preference for pearls set off a pearl fever when she toured America in 1926, and costume jewelers were quick to capitalize on that happy event. It was reported that Her Majesty wore three strands of precious pearls, pearl earrings, and a pearl necklace coiled several times around her wrist as a bracelet. Orienta advertised its merchandise as the "Aristocrat of Artificial Pearls"; necklaces had names like "Riviera," "Deauville," "Ritz," and "Fifth Avenue."

Pearls were worn front and back (opposite page)—even under the chin (below). Elaborate rhinestone clasps and tiny pearls were common features of bracelets (center).

Marchesa Casati (top), a celebrated trendsetter, favored the knee-length pearl sautoir.

Flo Ziegfeld, master of the Ziegfeld Follies chorus girls, claimed costume pearls were ideal for his "pearls of American girls." Singer Eddie Cantor touched another kind of appeal with his 1926 pitch, "Even the poor working girl who can only afford to shop at Woolworth's or Kresge's will have some kind of a strand of pearls around her neck." Poor and working she might have been, but a pearl necklace, even a fake, helped her live the glamorous life.

There were pearls at a price every girl could afford. A typist, salaried at $20 per week, could get a simple pearl strand from Woolworth's for 10 cents. "Lustrous" fakes could be mail-ordered from the Montgomery Ward's catalog: in 1927, their top-of-the-line imitation, pink "Bahama" pearls with a 10-carat gold spring ring clasp (made by Richelieu pearls) cost $8.50 for 60 inches. (Comparatively, a wool ladies' coat was $16.98.) The Saks Fifth Avenue department store offered their best-quality imitation pearls for $35 per strand, sold at the fine-jewelry counter.

At a vacation resort it was perfectly acceptable for rich women to wear fake pearls—only, of course, if they had the real necklace back home in the vault. The wealthy weren't above slipping in a few artificial pearls to make a necklace more spectacular, either. The American socialite Mrs. Statesbury was known to have slipped a few fakes into her Cartier pearl necklace. A fashion writer commented about her mixing fakes with the real: "It was hard to tell where Cartier stopped and Woolworth's began." Another ploy was to put a clasp set with real diamonds on a string of fake pearls. That way, a closer look at the clasp wouldn't give away the secret of the phony pearls.

The 1920s were host to conflicting fashion trends, but the pearl sautoir was a constant, a style that predates World War I. The couturiers of the early teens, notably Paul Poiret, used the dramatic swag of a tasseled pearl necklace and a feather aigrette or towering turban to create a long, tall silhouette for women. Even more theatrical was the pearl necklace that grazed the knees. The super-long pearl sautoir (falling to waist, hips, knees) survived until the late 1920s, when, signaled by a yawn from *Vogue* in the summer of 1929, necklaces were pruned. Said *Vogue*, "A long strand of even the most beautiful pearls looks poor, skimpy, and old-fashioned today." Readers were alerted to the new style—chokers and short triple strands of graduated beads. Both versions complemented the new necklines, the shallow round neck of evening dresses and the V-neck of daytime clothes and sportswear. However, the long necklace didn't die out altogether; it was still worn to balance formal evening gowns, with their floating drapery, tiers, panels, and scarf necklines.

Fashion had another way to get that stylish bulk. French couturier Lucien Lelong introduced multi-strand seed-pearl necklaces for the fall of 1928. The style caught on, and soon dozens of 30-inch strands of tiny pearls were braided into a single thick rope necklace. This necklace was paired with sweaters, suits, and afternoon outfits as well as evening gowns, an unusual versatility for a single necklace.

Due to the influence of the primitive "barbaric" style, costume jewelry's scale became larger in the late 1920s. The fake pearl's ladylike size changed; pearls as big as bird's eggs, often made of heavy solid glass, could be seen on the best necks. Pearls also came in rougher textures (baroque, fancy-cut melons, twists) and oddball shapes (oblong, tubular, square).

For those women with a fine-tuned fashion sense, fluctuations in the length of pearls, as well as the clasp, were worth tracking. The combination of low-cut evening dresses and short haircuts left the neck and the back bare. The necklace clasp became a new focal point, jazzed up with a heavy dose of pearls and rhinestones. Even the most pedestrian pearls had clasps or spring rings in solid 10- or 14-carat gold, or sterling silver, sometimes even set with a tiny diamond chip. No clasp was required for the cheap, 60-inch or longer necklaces.

Pearls pretty much stuck to their own kind of sophistication. For instance, they wouldn't be mixed with sporty wooden beads. It was big fashion news in 1926 when Lelong strung a few amber or tortoise beads on either side of a clasp, filling out the rest of the necklace with pearls. Pearls, crystals, and rhinestones were fashion "neutrals" that mingled with colored stones or each other. The mix of stones and pearls was an innovation either started or popularized by Chanel around 1927 and a classic style ever since. Chanel is credited with combining lengths of pearls spiked with a few semi-precious beads or stones, or their glass imitations.

Always sensitive to fashion, pearls began to mimic voguish colors. The late 1920s pronounced the suntan chic, a radical idea that sent women scurrying outdoors or after sunlamps and brown make-up.

Reportedly, Coco Chanel was one of the first fashionables to sport a suntan, which she picked up sailing on the Duke of Westminster's yacht. Sometime before Coco, dancer Josephine Baker was the toast of Paris, and her natural caramel coloring made a tan something to be desired. Another period story had an East Indian princess wearing a short skirt—and no stockings!—to a Paris restaurant. Her bare brown legs caused a shocking sensation, inspiring silk stockings in "suntan beige" (pre-suntan, only black or white stockings were worn).

The Duchess of Penaranda was the personification of the new tan chic, lyrically described by fashion photographer Cecil Beaton: "A Spanish beauty who appeared wearing a short white tunic with a deep scooped neckline and a skirt that stretched barely to the knees. She wore sunburn stockings with white satin shoes whose Spanish spike heels were fully six inches high. Her hair, brillianteened to a satin brilliance, was drawn back as tightly as a bullfighter's. The Duchess's complexion matched her stockings, for she was burned by the sun to a deep shade of iodine. Two enormous rows of pearl teeth were bared in a white, vital grin, complementing the half a dozen rows of pearls as large as pigeon's eggs that hung about her neck."

With suntanned goddesses like the Duchess, the ubiquitous brown—and

---

ARTIFICIAL PEARLS Along with their creation of champagne and foie gras, the French should be celebrated for the making of artificial pearls. Sometime during the mid-seventeenth century, a French rosary-bead maker, Jacquin, first dipped beads of either alabaster or glass into an iridescent paste—called essence d'Orient—made from fish scales. Artificial pearls have been made much the same way ever since: a cheap pearl is coated with a single layer of pearl essence, a better grade gets thirty to forty layers. Between the application of each layer, the pearl is polished with a chamois cloth and powder. Just like that of a real pearl, the beauty of the fake comes from the reflected luster of these multiple silken layers.

Today, when pearl luster is "natural," it is made from the scales of the unglamorous sardine or herring. Since the mid 1970s, polyester has been the ingredient that gives artificial pearls a pearly look.

There have been other types of pearls besides the dipped, some more dubious-looking than dazzling. In the early 1900s "Roman" pearls were popular, made by spraying the essence inside a hollow glass bead, then filling it up with wax. How to spot this type? A pencil tip held to the surface of a Roman pearl will cast a shadow inside the pearl bead.

all its variations—became the fashionable color for sportswear, gloves, shoes, handbags, and jewelry. In 1928 costume jewelers created "sunburn pearls" in shades of beige, brownish pink, and bronze, giving them the most exotic names imaginable: "Demi-Sumatra," "Sudan," and "Lido Sand."

Once suntan pearls had conquered color, the stage was set for an even more improbable innovation—polychrome pearls. The fashion that firmly fixed pearls with faux color was the frock of tiny print fabric. The geometrics, florals, and "jazz dots," and the loud clashing patterns and colors of these dresses needed a jewelry equal. Costume jewelry responded with its own charming novelty: pearls in colors like strawberry pink, lemon yellow, chartreuse, orchid, gray, green, and blue. No mistaking these pearls for the oyster's offspring! The couturier Molyneux brought out "gunmetal" pearls in 1927; the American Coro Company made gray "Pussywillow Pearls" in 1928. A huge success, colored pearls were worn by young and old and in dozens of necklace strands by wealthy women and working girls. Fine jewelers went on record bitterly complaining that these colorful fakes had trashed the real-pearl market.

Just when it seemed as if there was nothing new under the sun for pearls, there was another breakthrough. In the spring of 1927 *Women's Wear Daily* first reported the invention of phosphorescent pearls. Soon afterward Maison Schneider of Paris invented scented pearls, which gave off a whiff of rose, violet, or jasmine, guaranteed to last two months.

As bracelets, costume pearls didn't have much glory. Most bracelets were undistinguished little two- and three-strand arrangements that slipped or hooked on around the wrist. However, once the long sautoir fell from favor, women wrapped these out-of-style pearls around their upper arm or wrist. Worn on the wrist, the necklace joined the crowd—there was no shyness about putting on pearls with metal or other bracelets. Curiously, pearls would never be mixed with other necklaces in the same way around the neck.

Like the long and longer-still pearl necklaces, pearl earrings were also taken to exaggerated lengths. Most popular were large dewdrop earrings, pearls clustered at the end of tiny chains, and pendant drops. More elaborate was the three-pearl girandole earring, inspired by an eighteenth-century original. Long, dangling earrings were shown to their best advantage by the neat, short-cropped bobbed hair of the 1920s. With the head-hugging cloche, the pearl button earring (a perennial favorite) was more compatible.

Pearl earrings weren't necessarily worn conventionally. In 1926 there was a fad for wearing just one pearl earring. Another stylish gimmick, mismatched earrings, was attributed to Chanel: a black pearl graced one ear, a white pearl the other.

Oriental fan and pearls create a period still life.

Napoleon's wife, the Empress Eugénie (above, left) held court in France during the mid 1800s. Exotic bead and metal costume jewelry by Napier (left) was associated with fiery Spain and the tango. Tiny temple d'amour clips (below) reflect the influence of the skyscraper, a new phenomenon in the 1920s.

Rococo to Victoriana

The roster of romantics who inspired this jewelry includes Marie Antoinette, the Empress Eugénie of France, wife of Napoleon III, and the reigning queen of the tango, La Argentina. Costume jewelry knock-offs of Napoleon's finery puts his name on the list too.

Gold metal was the material of choice for these pieces, usually in a delicately tarnished, dull "antique" tone, or pink gold. Gold was the precious metal associated with royalty—the quintessential romantics. And fashion made gold the right choice for accessories, since its color complemented the stylish brown and beige clothing of the 1920s.

From Eugénie came typically Rococo motifs: garlands and swags, bowknots, cupids, lovebirds perched on a branch or fountain, acanthus leaves, bunches of grapes, urns, baskets, and jardinières overflowing with fruit and flowers. The influences of the Empress Eugénie and Marie Antoinette were closely linked: Eugénie admired Queen Marie's style, adopting elements associated with her reign and making them her own design motifs. One such example was Marie Antoinette's home, Versailles. In her honor, the *temple d'amour* (a tiny pavilion located on the grounds of Versailles) became a jewelry ornament. In the 1920s the ultrafashionable interior decorator Elsie de Wolfe, whose château was located on the grounds of Versailles, can be credited with popularizing the *temple d'amour* pin. Of course Elsie's pin was from Cartier and it did not go unnoticed. In 1927 a costume jewelry version, done in baguette-cut rhinestones, appeared, available to one and all for lots less than the Cartier original. Variations of *temple d'amour* jewelry were made with carved stones; some looked like pagodas, others were reminiscent of the stepped silhouettes of the new skyscrapers.

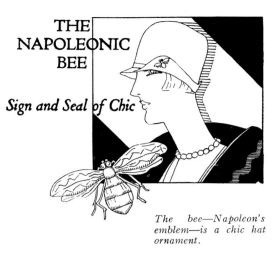

The bee—Napoleon's emblem—is a chic hat ornament.

The royal bee (above) was a favorite for small gold metal pins. Blue glass necklace (below) combines the opulence of the romantic style with the simplicity of the 1920s silhouette.

Marie Antoinette's fabled love for the pastoral also found its way into 1920s romantic jewelry. Enameled pins, sometimes set with tiny stones, recalled the dairy barn where the queen played milkmaid and usually featured a temple with a footbridge, a mill in a park, or a tiny house with a blooming tree.

Other Rococo jewelry favorites that were revisited included the tiny jewel-studded orange tree growing in a tub (influenced by both Versailles and East India) and the rose. The rose motif was popular throughout the 1920s and was part of the signature logo of the 1925 Exposition Internationale des Arts Décoratifs et Industriels Modernes in Paris. In 1929 Coco Chanel took the rose from its romantic garden, stiffly carved its petals into glass beads, and strung them together in a necklace. (The rose-cut bead necklace was an interesting departure in jewelry design for Chanel, since most of her pieces until this time had consisted of geometrically cut stones or simple brooches and buckles.)

Napoleon handed down his laurel leaves to the 1920s. A flexible chain of linked leaves was editioned by the Napier Company in gold metal for their "Empire" jewelry collection of 1927. And Napoleon's royal insignia, the bee, became a smart gold pin, priced at a not-cheap $2.50. This simple, streamlined laurel-leaf jewelry can be recognized as the ancestor of the later "tailored" jewelry popular with the wool suits that began to be regarded as suitable daytime wear for women in the late 1920s.

While the demure suit might have been fine for day, tango dressing was the look for evening. It was a wild counterpoint completely in keeping with the flapper's romantic fantasy. The tango, introduced around 1915, was still daring enough to shock and fashion pounced on it. New York store ads burbled, "Who says it's an old Spanish custom to wear lace and much of it . . . it's as New as the Paris openings!" In the name of the tango, women wore black lace, vibrant red, and "tango orange." They carried lace fans and wrapped themselves in flowered, fringed shawls. Towering hair combs, made of tortoiseshell or plastic studded with rhinestones, were bound to their heads with bands. In Paris the tango queen La Argentina thrilled nightclub crowds. "Tango" was the slang word for feeling upbeat. The jewelry to match this heavy-breathing image was a perfect fit: intricate, lacy filigree metal set with flat, square-cut slabs of yellow glass "topaz." The color of honey, this "topaz" was a long-standing 1920s favorite. Its odd color, creating a striking effect, had been copied from real jewelry, where yellow diamonds, citrines, and pale emeralds had been popular since around 1914, associated with Japanese art and the Fauve painters' wild color experiments. Earrings for the tango were dangling, circular hoops or pendants quivering with tiny metal beads. The Coro Company created glass topaz "Rio Rita" jewelry, capitalizing on the Ziegfeld Follies stage hit of the same name.

Costume jewelry companies zeroed in on the tango's exotic appeal: "Spanish topaz is 'le dernier cri' in France, and 'the last word' in America . . . it makes you think of a languorous, romantic, olive-skinned Madridian beauty doing a sublime Spanish tango," went an ad in *Women's Wear Daily* in 1927. Along with topaz, jet was a material considered suitably "Spanish." Costume jewelry used glass, Bakelite, or composition plastic as a look-alike for the too-expensive real jet.

The romantic impulse expanded jewelry's palette, popularizing a range of blues. Blue was a color associated with a real-life royal romance: Queen Mary of England chose sapphires for her engagement ring. French couturier Jeanne Lanvin made "Lanvin blue" her signature color, reportedly inspired by a certain shade in a Fra Angelico painting. The Coro Company originated true-blue jewelry, claiming "grotto blue jewelry was a 'Rhapsody in Blue' no less compelling than the melody George Gershwin's genius has made famous." And pale parma violet, pale blue, and absinthe green were declared by fashion to be the right colors for jewelry stones for the Riviera and Palm Beach during resort season.

The romantic style of jewelry may seem to be an oddity, given the 1920s fever for hard, modern shapes and sleek surfaces. But romantic jewelry followed fashion: the short flapper "tube" dresses coexisted with the full-skirted "robe de style" and the ladylike flounced silk tea frock.

Victorian-revival jewelry fit perfectly with these girlish dresses. Anything associated with the Victorians—once scorned as hopelessly old fashioned by the snappy flappers—was back in fashion in the late 1920s. Stylish women now took eagerly to Grandma's cameo. Cameos were used for brooches, bracelets, earrings—even sautoirs were made of tiny linked cameos. Though their recognition was a bow to tradition, cameos weren't always treated with traditional respect: in composition plastic, cameos became giant, oversized pendants worn on chains or ribbons.

A set of "Spanish" jewelry by Napier, made up in antique-looking gold metal.

ARCHAEOLOGICAL INFLUENCES

While it was the hand of a bold archaeologist that lifted the lid of King Tutankhamen's sarcophagus, fashion's hand put Egypt's motifs—hieroglyphics, scarabs, pyramids—onto a thousand elegant trifles. Just a few of these included umbrella handles, vanity sets, letter openers, ashtrays, cigarettes, perfumes ("Nuit d'Egypte"), face powder, golden sandals, and, of course, jewelry.

The romance of this tomb robbery in 1922 launched a "Tut mania" for anything and everything Egyptian, from fashions to home furnishings. Tut's curse gave women the fashionable shivers. The stylish femme fatale dreamed of herself as a slave girl, concubine, or queen of the Nile. She called her "beau" by a new name—"sheik."

Besides King Tut, there was real-life inspiration for this rash of exoticism. For example, *Harper's Bazar* [sic] featured a charming and true vignette about exotic Russian dancer Ida Rubenstein. Ida, *Bazar* said, was a "brilliant example" who traveled the North African desert with an amazing wardrobe. "Her hunting costume was made of thin white kid and her hunting helmet might have been designed for a Princess of the *Mille et une Nuits*. Trousered and helmeted with gold she looked up at the starry night from her tent door. Clad in woven silks—Worth made this hunting trousseau—she reclined on leopard skins in the twilight of her desert shelter, her jewels like sparks of fire in the shadows."

In Paris, fashion chronicler and poet Jean Cocteau meowed about women in his diary: "[they] . . . wish to be transformed into Egyptian dancing girls, silk and fur furniture covers, lampshades, cushions in the harem of the sultan à la mode." Those stay-at-home "lampshade" Cleopatras, who couldn't visit the land of the Nile, could still share the fantasy with fashionable items that had Egyptian motifs. And nothing took to the Egyptian look more readily than jewelry. Both costume and precious jewelry plugged into the style: the mummy, asp, sphinx, obelisk, lily, scarab, soul-birds, the jackal-headed god, ibis, the figure of the pharaoh, and the pharaoh's crook staff were all popular design elements, incorporated into pendants, bracelets, brooches, earrings, even buttons. Hieroglyphics, scribbled geometrics, and the pyramid's severe triangle were translated into geometrical patterns, set as a design feature or border on rhinestone brooches, flexible bracelets, and earrings.

It all happened very quickly, too: no sooner had Tutankhamen's mummy been yanked from his tomb than there was a flood of Nile jewelry. In 1923 a Napier Company press release extolled its "jewelry with the spirit of ancient Egypt. A complete line of stunning necklaces, brooches, bracelets, and earrings, in the vivid colors and designs made popular by the interest in the excavation of the tomb of Tutankhamen."

Generally, land-of-the-Nile costume jewelry was skinny, dangly, and delicate, made of brightly colored glass beads, lengths of gold chain, odd amulets, or chunky slabs of pseudo-lapis crawling with pseudo-Egyptian religious and

Bright red and green glass necklace (above) has all the Egyptian trappings—mummies, scarabs, hieroglyphics. More Egyptology (opposite page)—a flexible gold metal snake bracelet with glass eyes.

symbolic figures and hieroglyphics. Mixing cultures, an Egyptian-style neck-lace often had a floppy "Oriental" tassel at one end; Egyptian amulets and pen-dants were also strung on "Oriental" silk cords and ribbons. Not so strangely, the massive jeweled Egyptian collar didn't figure in this revival; it was too wide and too heavy and couldn't be worn with the high necklines or the fragile fabrics of 1920s clothing. Both necklaces and earrings were long, spare, and dangling, mixing beads in tiers.

How to tell if a piece is costume jewelry, Egyptian-style? If it doesn't have a telltale scarab, mummy, or scrap of hieroglyphics, check the color. While the cool Art Deco color scheme of black-and-white and silver is the 1920s Egyptian precious jewelry standard (onyx, diamonds, and platinum were used for the real thing), costume jewelry followed the original Egyptians' palette, more or less: turquoise, lapis, red carnelian, pink quartz, and black onyx were copied in glass or composition matrix, used alone or in various combinations with one another. Green "jade" or "jasper" also was sometimes added. Like the Egyptians, cos-tume jewelers used gold metal, calling it "Nile gold."

The cobra and the asp were fashionable jewelry pets, reproduced in slinky gold "snake" chains to coil around wrist, throat, and pinky finger. The snake chain was made with and without the serpent head. The chain alone was always associated with "Egypt"; occasionally it was also set with vibrant Egyptian col-ored stones or beads. Sometimes this jewelry did have the cobra's head, with

fanged mouth open and angry ruby-chip eyes. A variation was the cobra with its tail in its mouth. Sleek and simple as a whip, the snake chain has become a timeless and standard jewelry motif.

A travel writer, circa 1923, offered his romantic insight into the appeal of Egyptomania: "To woman, there is a primitive barbarism in the desert, a savage tang in the fierce stare of the Bedouin, which strips from her the veneer of civilization and lends the forgotten excitement of the old days when men fought and died for her possession." Stretched a little, that "savage tang" popularized another fad—the "slave" or "scarabee" bracelet. Slave bracelets were made with all sizes of scarabee beetles, though the formula was always the same: round scarab beetles, in glass or composition, mimicking semi-precious stones. The scarabs had wings etched on top of their bodies, hieroglyphics etched on their bellies, and they were joined together by golden links into a flexible bracelet. The slave bracelet was also made with domed cabochon stones—or square, rectangular, or octagonal glass links—in the same colors, or combinations of colors. Bracelets were also worn "slave style" as a narrow bangle on the arm above the elbow. Long after the Tut tomb frenzy died down, the slave bracelet has been periodically resurrected.

Amulet necklace by Napier (above) depicts an Egyptian pharaoh. Seeds, glass, and wooden beads are the materials of the rough scarab necklace at right.

'Le Captif'
BRACELET

Ordained as the vogue of the moment at Biarritz, Deauville, and the Lido. Its instant popularity is not comparable to anything in recent years, and nowhere has the spirit of its inception been so alluringly captured, or more faithfully rendered, than in this newest CK product, the Le Captif bracelet.

Slave Bracelets
Latest Fashionable Style

Gold
Filled
and
Sterling
Silver

$1 65

Slave bracelet is the last word in fashionable. The are being worn by women everywhere. It difficult to select a gift for her that would be ly appreciated and give more happiness than this. g fastener.

33B—Gold filled $1.65
340—Sterling silver 1.65
Postage, 3¢ extra

*ve bracelets were the emblem of chic—for
men and men (popularized by Rudolph
entino). The assorted scarab bracelets (far
t) are of metal and composition plastic.*

Oddly, fashion didn't adopt Egyptian themes as strongly as jewelry did. However, *Vogue* announced in spring 1923: "Pleating was never better—and that's Egyptian. Tiered skirts are seen—and they're Egyptian." Fashion's only apparent cribbing from the Egyptians was this pleating, the straight-as-an-arrow dress, and the clingy sheaths of couturier Vionnet, which later came into their own in the 1930s (although they were then retitled "Grecian" gowns).

The Egyptian look did guide beauty, boosted by the newly popular suntan craze. "Novelty in makeup . . . called Egyptian . . . a heavy coat of tan, which is in reality put on with a brown powder. The fancy for the Orient is seen also in the manner in which eyes are penciled in almond shape and lashes are heavily beaded," reported the *New York Times* fashion page in 1927.

No excavation site was left untouched; fashion's fancy flitted to the contents of other tombs later in the decade. Jewelry motifs were plundered from discoveries in Mexico and Guatemala. The Mayan and Aztec Indians, and the American Navajo Indians, gave jewelry the repetitious, rhythmic patterns that were associated with Art Deco. These bold, direct shapes had a high primitivism that the 1920s translated into decorative elements. The zigzag, the step-pattern tiers (also called "skyscraper" by the moderns), and stripes were used on accessories (cigarette cases, vanity cases), as well as on jewelry. Costume jewelry borrowed from the Indians' color palette—delicate tints of green, yellow, silver, and pink gold. Rougher stuff—hammered metal platework and savagely carved beads—also lent inspiration to barbaric jewelry. Novelty jewelry profited from the Indians' art, too. Modeled after the Indians' little gold figures and stone carvings, "grotesque" ornaments of jaguars, lizards, birds, butterflies, and vultures populated the land of 1920s jewelry, and would recur in the 1940s.

ORIENTAL INSPIRATION

No stranger to the exotic, the stylish woman of the 1920s was steeped in the spirit of the Orient—India, China, and Japan. She simpered, dressed like a harem beauty or a geisha, and was the very vision of fashionable allure. A contemporary observer wrote, "the women . . . looked as though they were acting in a fairy tale: Schéhérazade, Sâlomé, Salommbô, Oriental ladies from rich harems. They went by in sumptuous pyjamas of silk or figured velvet, brilliantly colored, glittering with sequins and stones. Fantasy reigned, at its wildest." Though it sounds like the description of a costume party, these were ladies dressed for lunch in 1926. Real costume parties were even more flamboyant. Paul Poiret, French couturier and something of a public-relations genius, linked himself with the Oriental craze. He threw a "Thousand and Second Night" party for three hundred Persian-costumed guests, complete with dancing girls, slaves, and monkeys in chains. Poiret described another of his famous parties, the "Nouveaux Riches": "All the ladies had to wear silver or gold, and silver coins were heaped upon the tables in the garden . . . the golden rain of fireworks filled the air. Dozens of oysters were given away and each one contained a string of pearls . . . ." Fashionable hostesses in Paris, London, New York—even suburban Connecticut—were fired with copycat enthusiasm for their own Persian theme parties. The distinction between fashionable dress, stage costumes, and costume party get-ups was faint. It was at this edge that a sensibility was created, where the fantasy of the Oriental world was translated into the luxe and decadent style of the 1920s. And jewelry was just as dazzlingly, dizzyingly lavish.

Aladdin's lamp was a beacon for jewelry. Like time bandits, the fashionable bejeweled themselves as if they'd burgled some sultan's gem vaults. A *Harper's Bazaar* writer noted the scene at a casino in 1928: " . . . jewels like a thug's dream of Paradise. Diamond necklaces that make Marie Antoinette look like a prize in a Christmas cracker. Enormous emerald pendants carved—perhaps with the name of Allah? Fabulous stones on fragile fingers. Bracelets clanking from wrist to elbow. Elaborate earrings sweeping scented shoulders."

The fascination with the Orient started in the early 1900s. In 1911 King George V of England was crowned Emperor of India, with attendant pomp, circumstance, and homage from the bejeweled maharajahs and princes. Jacques Cartier, of the Cartier jewelry firm, traveled to the Persian Gulf in search of gems and inspiration. Another Indian influence came by way of the ballet *Schéhérazade*, premiered by the Ballets Russes in the spring of 1910. Its brilliant costumes and sets sent stylish shock waves through fashion, interior design, fabrics, graphic design, and jewelry.

Precious jewelry and costume jewelry alike took their cues from the color rainbow of *Schéhérazade*. Until that time, since the heyday of Art Nouveau, fashion's colors had been harmonious, timid, subdued. Poiret described the old colors, and generously credited himself with the change: "The dim thighs of nymphs, the lilacs, and the swooning colors, mallow, wishy-washy blue, Nile

Galalith plastic pendant (above) resembles jade. The silk necklace cord was considered "Oriental."

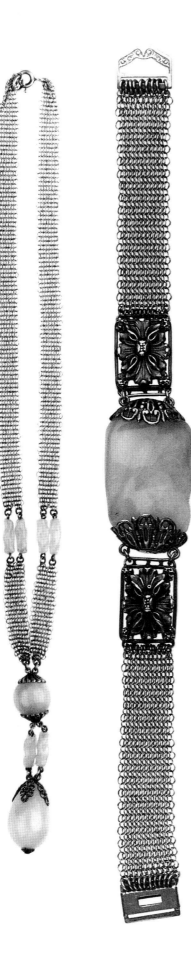

green and straw yellow, everything that was smooth, washed-out and insipid was to the fore. Now I have let some wolves into the sheepfold, those lively reds, greens, purples and blues make all the rest sit up . . . ." From these influences, jewelry borrowed the riot of color and new colors put together in new ways (notably green, black, white, and red). In 1925, at the Paris Palais Galliera exhibition, the trendsetting precious jewelry was made up in the very Oriental color trio of green, black, and white in emeralds, onyx, diamonds. Indian and Persian gemstones and enamel work inspired the use of colors like lapis, turquoise, sharp orange, yellow, emerald green, sapphire blue, amethyst, purple, and violet, deep coral, and lacquer red. Revolutionary colors for jewelry, they were used in revolutionary combinations: blue was paired with green, amethyst with blue or green, coral with black. Green, red, blue, and white made a popular combination. Cool "neutrals" such as clear glass, rock crystal, and pearls were set with these flamboyant stone combinations. Black was a favored color accent, incorporated into tubes, roundels, and beads. By 1929 jewel colors had been tamed: the pure white of diamonds copied in rhinestones became the style that dominated the 1930s.

The way color was integrated into jewelry changed, too. Until about 1920 the color contrasts in jewelry were created by enamel lines on border designs. Now, calibré stones (stones cut in various shapes to create a design) provided the color for borders or ornamental shapes.

Carved and etched stones—especially those in ruby red and emerald green—were Indian-inspired. Oblong and round stones were etched with lengthwise stripes, the melon cut, so called because it resembled a cantaloupe's markings. Costume jewelry took up this distinctive cut and got creative, "melonizing" crystal, glass, metal, wood, composition, and pearl beads. Couturier Jean Patou introduced a costume jewelry variation on the cut bead in 1929, maybe never duplicated: a necklace of big wooden beads covered with fabric, which was pleated to look like melon cuts. The many-branched tree of life (symbol of the garden of Eden) and the calligraphy of India were also design elements that decorated pendants and were etched into beads.

Necklace and bracelet set (above) of silver metal and green glass-imitation jade. Black metal bracelet (right) brilliantly enameled with chinoiserie figures.

The teens and 1920s were wild for tassels! Big ones, little ones, all sizes were sent swinging from clothing and accessories (scarves, capes, coats, umbrellas, fans) and furniture (lampshades, chair covers, cushions). Poiret, with his mania for the Oriental look, championed the tassel as a decorative element: necklaces of skinny silk cords ending with a tassel, others, the width of a hand span, were worn as belts. The Islamic art of Morocco had an influence felt in Paris since the colony came under the French protectorate in 1911. (The tassel and the bowknot had both been in and out of favor since the seventeenth century. They were popular with Marie Antoinette and the Empress Eugénie, the wife of Napoleon III, in the late 1800s.) From India came the tasseled turban ornament of pearls and beads. Redone the 1920s way, the dangly drop of tasseled beads became the period's number-one motif. The tassel and its thousand variations were used as a shoulder ornament, as well as for pendants, necklaces, and earrings: "Very chic is a long tassel of tiny brilliants, almost touching the shoulders," noted the *New York Times* in 1929. "The tassel earring is shown in many lengths and variations of stones—but the longer the earring, the more fashionable at the moment." Earlier, in 1921, *Vogue* gave the long earring its nod: "One out of every three women seen in the Parc or the Bois, lunching at the Ritz or dancing at the Ambassador wore earrings an inch or two in length." Earrings dangled linked flower blossoms, bell shapes, or bunches of grapes, sometimes ending with a drop cabochon. Rhinestones also adapted to the style; long waterfalls occasionally glittered down to a stone of a different color.

By late 1929 the Oriental fad had passed, although the tassel was still around. Fashion writers, ever in search of the new, claimed the tassel was fresh again, suited to the swaying fringe drapery of the new dress styles.

Even at the peak of the King Tut craze, the stylistic potpourri included fashion from Japan and China. In 1923 the theme of the Paris Opéra ball was China. Suddenly popular were "kimono wrappers" and "coolie" and "Confucius" coats. French couturier Doeuillet dubbed a dress "pagoda," because of its pointed hem, flaring tiers, and amusing little Chinese character motifs embroidered in colored threads.

Delicate Oriental glass ornament worn on a fine necklace chain (above). The tasseled pearl necklace (right) was a 1920s signature ornament.

SEMI-PRECIOUS STONES With their exotic tang of the Orient, semi-precious stones were the bridge between precious and costume jewelry. Considered slightly daring or avant-garde, their effect was noted by *Vogue* in 1928, "When she wears semi-precious jewelry of the current mode . . . she ranks herself with the modernists." Semi-precious jewelry was originally called "costume" jewelry. Jewelry of non-precious materials (such as Bakelite) was called "novelty," a term used in the late 1800s and early 1900s. It was only in the mid-1920s that "costume" jewelry replaced the "novelty" title.

Couturier Jean Patou made jewelry history in 1927 when he passed out a pamphlet at his collection showing to denounce costume jewelry in favor of semi-precious stones. He designed "robes à bijoux" (jeweled dresses) that had ornaments specially made for them—brooches and long chains of amethysts, aquamarines, and topaz—in collaboration with jeweler Jean Fouquet.

The Buddha (above) was a popular motif for costume jewelry—shown here, a pendant. Carved wooden and glass beads (below) strung on a necklace cord.

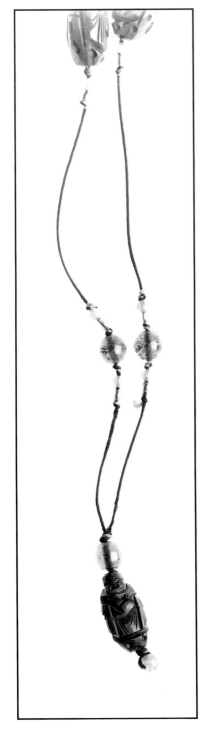

China and Japan's gifts to jewelry were jade, lacquer, bone, horn, and ivory, the materials resurrected from Art Nouveau. Motifs included the dragon, the plum blossom, the crane, the pagoda, and Oriental calligraphy. Souvenir coins, and symbolic and lucky pieces were also popular. What jewelry to wear with Chinese fashions? There was plenty to choose from. Japanese and Chinese ethnic jewelry, available in Paris in 1923, was admired and copied. Jade—both white and green—was happily re-created in costume jewelry in composition plastic, even to its slightly mottled and streaked coloring. Pendants of colored glass, composition plastic, and imitation tortoise were decorated with birds, Buddhas, dragons, flowers. Souvenir jewelry—Oriental coins and pierced disks (the "pi" disk, with a center hole, was a symbol of the heavens)—was scribbled with real or real-looking calligraphy, and threaded on a silk neck cord or bracelet. "Jade" was also carved into tiny good-luck elephants for bracelets and pendants (gamblers in resorts like Monte Carlo loved them). The seated Buddha figure, the pot-bellied Japanese god of happiness, and the hand of the Buddha were also popular motifs.

Eastern influences became part of the creative free-for-all that mixed styles and motifs; for instance, a carved green-glass emerald, typically Oriental, would be set in a piece of romantic jewelry, such as a fruit basket, or used as the eye of a novelty animal pin. Costume jewelry took liberties with Oriental motifs. It knocked them off in oddball materials, colors, and combinations that didn't resemble the precious original model in the least little bit—but the spirit of the East was there.

Madama Nazimova

Of colored pearls on lamé was this exotic headdress worn by Madame Nazimova, the actress, with a coat of heavy brocade embroidered with jewels.

Madame Yteb

Madame Yteb, the dress designer, wore a periwinkle blue turban with pearls and ostrich plumes in two shades. Coat of silver lamé over dress of blue tulle and diamonds.

THE BARBARIC LOOK

On the sidelines of Art Deco's stark, geometric reign lurked a sullen outcast: barbaric jewelry. Like its namesake, this jewelry was boldly oversized, usually made from primitive, natural materials (wood, cork, shells), and looked as if it could have been put together by a child. Simple as a string of wooden beads, the barbaric was a powerful new fashion statement.

The woman identified with barbaric jewelry was the original "wild thing," Nancy Cunard. A spoiled, rich, scandal-prone socialite, so skinny she was described by one wit as "an asparagus," she could have more accurately been called "an asparagus with bracelets," since she was never without her trademark wrist-to-elbow ivory bangles. The rattle of Nancy's ivory armloads signaled a warning—elegance, beware!

In its way, barbaric jewelry was like Mr. Wrong: it was rude, crude, and had an ill-mannered look about it. In Nancy Cunard's case, it was sometimes too noisy. The clean gleam of pearls, the narrow brilliance of stones didn't suit her. A rebel, she wore jewelry that was definitely not new, not pretty, and might just be dirty. In her day, she was never cited by fashion magazines as a trendsetter, but Nancy's style was prophetic: the fresh, raw audacity of her big clunky bracelets, necklaces that looked as if they were hewn from logs and or broken boulders or snatched from the jaws of big game animals, were a rival to rhinestones.

The barbaric represented a turning away from the cool perfection, and what came to be the negative associations, of Art Deco and stood instead for the anti-precious sentiment in jewelry. "Barbaric jewelry shows the rush back to the natural, avoidance of the artificial so characteristic of war fashions," noted a jewelry publication in 1928. It wasn't an easy style to love; the *New York Times* called it "jewelry for the New Barbarians" in spring 1929.

Given the 1920s taste for the exotic, the extravagant, and the outlandish, barbaric jewelry's popularity was a natural. It was rooted in a sophisticated, intricate knit of elements stolen from African art, souvenir jewelry of Egypt and the South Seas, and from fairy tales set in the Far East.

Within a select circle in Paris, collecting African art was extremely fashionable. Nancy Cunard's apartment was decorated with African sculpture and fetishes—and hundreds of ivory bracelets, stacked on wooden poles. Artists such as Picasso and Modigliani also collected African art, lending it the cachet of the avant-garde.

The original barbarian, Nancy Cunard, photographed by Cecil Beaton in 1929. Fashion rebel, Nancy loaded down her arms with heavy ivory bracelets and bright wooden bangles.

In 1921, in Marseilles, an exhibition of primitive art from the French colonies was shown, and even earlier African sculpture had been exhibited in a small Paris gallery. This was at least ten years before barbaric/African elements were picked up in jewelry, but it was an influence that was "in the air." A major display of art and artifacts from the French colonies at the Colonial Exhibition in Paris in 1931 would have an even greater impact on both jewelry and fashions.

A bulletin sent from Paris to an American magazine attributed the trend to the Prince of Wales's safaris. "Five popular hunting enthusiasts went to Africa in search of big game. They sent back photos and sketches to Paris, 'note the jewels.' With the cult of Congo art a popular Paris fad, they (the photos) were used as a base for new fashions in jewelry that are strangely like what a native girl would choose for her costume."

How did the barbaric look invade civilization? As the flapper evolved into the modern girl, she became daring in a new way, a fearless Amazon in massive, heavy cuff bracelets and knuckle-covering big wooden rings who sported her jewelry like hunting trophies.

At its crudest, barbaric jewelry was made of the most primitive materials—shells, nuts, seeds, feathers, cork, elephant hair, leather, and wood. Metal was also used, molded into straight-from-the-mine nuggets strung into bracelets, hinged or made into one-piece cuffs. Precious materials—quartz, amber, tortoise, ivory, ebony, coral, turquoise, lapis—were copied in composition plastic and used in a natural, rough state: "Bits of rough turquoise are used in the new bracelets, like those seen on the wrists of Oriental potentates—gems strung together on elephant's hair . . . carried out in rough gems of all kinds, put together just as found, as if a large piece of gem had been broken up for use."

Just as the materials of barbaric jewelry were a throwback to simpler and savage times, so was its scale. Size was no object for the new barbarians. A jewelry magazine noted, "jewelry fashions in Paris today would lead one to believe that the craftsmen are all designing for a race of giants. Big massive pieces replace the delicate motifs. Necklaces are as big as bird's eggs; bracelets are wide bands of metal that look more as if they were the arm protection of a prehistoric warrior than the decoration of a feminine arm." Gargantuan jewelry complemented a woman's femininity in a strange way, "some women appear to be wearing gauntlets, their tiny pink hands peeping out from below the metallic wrist and forearm. . . . "

Necklaces grew to the same oversized scale as bracelets, but not in a wide, Egyptian-style collar, as might be expected. Necklaces couldn't shake the bead influence, so barbaric neck ornaments were big, almost comical circles of beads or rows of triangular "teeth."

The mummy's curse also hung in the air in the 1920s. King Tutankhamen's tomb was a continuing fantasy and a fashion inspiration. While Egyptian motifs were a runaway success for the fashion industry in the early and mid-1920s, its novelty eventually became all too familiar. The next wave of Egypt's influence

came as primitive souvenir artifacts—clumsy strings of mummy beads, curious amulets, odd and ugly trinkets—all of which lent their look to barbaric jewelry. Actual souvenirs from the grave were so popular that a jeweler's publication cautioned: "Well to make sure that mummy jewelry is disinfected. It should be sent to some proper establishment . . . the germs may still be alive after all these thousands of years, as some wearers of mummy beads have discovered. . . . "

From Egypt and Africa fashion restlessly looked to more remote corners for ideas. The "exotic" shifted from Egypt to the South Sea Islands, Java, and Hawaii. The jewelry these locations inspired was a 1920s dream of what the primitives should look like. Working from a fantasy concept, the styles of the jewelry were interchangeable—a "Tahitian" necklace looked just like a "Hawaiian" necklace.

Materials might have been basic, but their range of refinements was not. Take wooden jewelry, for example. Most American jewelry companies launched a line of exotica, a good deal of it wooden, in 1928–29. Wood was carved, gilded, or even covered with feathers. The Castlecliff Company offered beads and bracelets in amethyst wood, snake wood, African onyx wood, walnut, teak, rosewood, and ebony. Coro made "aloha" round wood chokers for $3.50, and as early as 1926 the company offered "spiked necklets of Javanese inspiration." Other choices included "Tahitian" (wooden beads with a waxed finish), "South Sea," and "Hawaiian" (carved wooden pineapples) jewelry. In 1929 couturier Norman Hartnell, who later dressed the British royal family, created a gold wood lei to pair with a dress inspired by Hawaiian costume.

Wood didn't stand alone: it was also combined with other materials, some of them unlikely, such as beads of crystal, glass, ivory, and amber. When it was painted, wood came in gay brights. Couturier Lucien Lelong's 1929 jewelry line was a rainbow: red, green, beige, bright blue, black, navy, and mutiple browns, in square, oblong, and round beads. Red was an especially popular color for summer jewelry in 1929, as it flattered a deep suntan. It was a 1920s hallmark to separate the beads with small roundels of metal or glass, or even rhinestone. This was a stylistic device as well as a practical one, to prevent the paint on the beads from chipping.

Nutmegs and beans (opposite page), were "barbaric" jewelry materials. A chunk of rough amber on a ribbon (above), makes a necklace. Short choker (below) of painted wood beads, two inches in diameter.

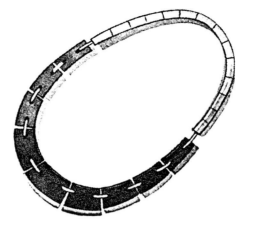

Rough-textured glass beads (above) were daringly primitive. Leather and metal linked into a big bracelet and collar necklace from the late 1920s (above, right). Short necklace (opposite page) combines bold-colored glass beads and metal "spearheads."

However it was used, wood was also a popular jewelry material because of fashion's dictate: in 1927 couture gave the nod to a color that would rule fashion for the next two years—brown. Brown was the color of choice for fabric that spring, brown reptile and alligator the material of choice for everything else that mattered (shoes, handbags, umbrella handles). Brown may have been the couturiers' way of thumbing their noses at the fine jewelers. As a *New York Times* fashion writer delicately pointed out, "No color presents such a problem for the jewelers." Brown killed the glitter of precious stones. Happily, brown wasn't such a problem for couturiers' jewelry. They solved this problem of their own making by using novel materials and colors for their costume jewelry: wood, of course, and tortoise, amber, topaz, and their imitations—the signature materials of the barbaric. Of course, fine jewelers wouldn't carry or create jewelry of such pedestrian materials, which put the couturiers right where they wanted to be—dictating fashion and the jewelry to wear with it.

Coco Chanel is rarely associated with the barbaric, but she did try her hand at it in the late 1920s. Curiously, her work in this style lacks the innovation and the distinctive voice that characterizes her other jewelry. *Women's Wear Daily* showed her "gypsy" necklace in 1929: a short, triple strand of red, green, and yellow wooden beads and pearls, priced at $5. Very ordinary. Other Chanel examples from that year were also undistinguished: necklaces of red stones strung on a wooden chain, large turquoise beads, or blue and green melon-cut beads, separated by tiny "wedding ring" roundels.

Clumsy, bulky cuff bracelets were in vogue for the first time around 1928–29. Always bold, Elsa Schiaparelli, Chanel's designing rival, did cuffs of alternating black-and-white flat rectangles out of ebony and ivory, strung on elastic, to be worn around wrist or ankle (the ankle version was worn at the beach). Same date, same idea, Lelong strung half circles of wood on elastic so they would stand up in a 3-D ruff around the wrist. Bracelets also came in hinged sections: flat plaques of wood, plain or carved, were joined by gold metal links. Big U-shaped cuff bracelets slipped on, their surfaces carved in relief.

It was one step from wood to nuts and seeds—as primitive as jewelry could get. Courageous Louiseboulanger, a minor French couturier, took the first step with this idea. The Saks Fifth Avenue store featured her "delightful necklaces made of twisted strands of wooden beads and exotic seeds, fastened with lumps of gold" in April 1929.

When metal was crafted into barbaric jewelry, it was usually gold metal and oversized. Even a delicate metal snake chain could turn uncivil at the hands of costume jewelers. Lelong made a fringe of snake chains that hung down like a hula dancer's grass skirt around the neck, wrist, and from the ears. Slave bracelets, too, took fashion prisoners: "Bracelets made of cubes of flat beaten gold for afternoon . . . worn like great shackles or fetters . . . with satin gowns, it is a look suitable for tea." Metal was also pounded into spearheads or primitive coins. In 1926 the American Napier Company created the "Viking" collection, which featured simple jewelry of coiled links, a look that would be revived some thirty years later. The French hat/jewelry designer Madame Agnès made herself a hulking, four-inch-wide gold cuff bracelet that caught all eyes. It had an unpleasant pitted texture and a knuckle-sized knob on top. Copied in the United States, advertisements heralded it as "the bracelet Madame Agnès wore at the Paris races, creating a furor!" The next year, the designer caught fashion's fancy again, with her "pipe organ" bracelet cuff. Madame was also seen with one arm bound by six huge bracelets—a couple of them no less than four inches wide.

For the timid who were not ready for the bracelet shackles of Madame Agnès, or a necklace of golf-ball-sized wooden beads, the barbaric language was translated into more ladylike jewelry. One of barbaric jewelry's motifs was the savage "tooth necklace." These triangular teeth and the way they were set—with a wide space separating each tooth—was interpreted in more delicate materials, such as glass and plastic. Even when made up in a more "civilized" material, barbaric jewelry still looked jagged and dangerous. Designers sometimes saved a step and made jewelry part of the dress: Louiseboulanger painted a tooth necklace right on the front of her black crêpe afternoon dress.

Though it looked crude and childishly savage next to the refinement of other types of 1920s jewelry, the barbaric also exemplified the period's worship of style. It must have been an extravagant, novel, and gleeful experience for a woman to pay $18.89 for an ultra-fashionable necklace made of seeds and shells, imported from Paris, when the same price would pay for a first-rate dress, all in real silk. That's civilization!

NOVELTY JEWELRY

Novelty jewelry represented the fads and fancies of the 1920s. Humor was its distinguishing feature; cartoony creatures (man and beast) and other whimsical objects were its subjects. Any material was fair game for this jewelry—from rhinestones to wood to plastic.

Tiny glass elements (above), hand-painted on the back so that the image is viewed through a transparent bubble, were used for "sports" jewelry.

Whimsy aside, novelty jewelry shared the more conservative family characteristics of 1920s costume jewelry. Pieces were streamlined, flatness was emphasized over 3-D modeling, and the jewelry was tiny. A combination of factors made this jewelry small-scale. Most of the novelty pieces were either earrings, pins, or stickpins used to ornament the tiny cloche hats in vogue, or pinned on a handbag. The small size of the jewelry also made it look almost precious—those tiny rhinestone-bedecked pins could almost pass for real diamonds. Most novelty jewelry was with pearls or pavé stones, or decorated with colored enamel.

Fads taken to humorous extremes pervaded the novelty market. For example, Charles Lindbergh's solo flight—the first—across the Atlantic in 1927 inspired a frenzy for souvenirs associated with flight and airplanes. Just a short time after the pilot landed in France, the Coro Company scrambled to commemorate the event, creating a Lindbergh airplane pin, enameled in red, white, and blue, and decorated with pearls and rhinestones. That wasn't all: airplane earrings began to dangle from ladies' earlobes. A jewelry magazine gave how-to's on the proper airborne fashion attitude. "Airplane earrings are worn as if the wearer were in flight. Short hair, worn off the ears, and an alert expression are said to be requirements for the young woman who would wear these new Paris novelties . . . ." Propellers and wings were also popular motifs for jewelry. For females with a total aviation fixation, there were even airplane hats to complete the outfit—felt beanies topped with floppy felt propellers.

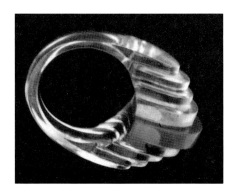

Fashion's radical offspring—sportswear—was created in the 1920s as a whole new category of clothing and an arena for stylish accessorizing that was adopted wholeheartedly by women and couturiers. The French tennis champion, Suzanne Lenglen, emerged in 1921 as the era's goddess of sportswear. Long, lean, and athletic, her look provided a role model; her knit tennis sweaters and short skirts were hailed as the new mode for dressing in the city, not just on the tennis courts. In their new togs, women were liberated to play tennis, play golf, drive a car. Sporty sweaters and dresses were ornamented and buckled with jewelry shaped like tennis rackets and golf clubs. Speed and motion were a preoccupation of the 1920s. Coupled with symbols of luxurious high life, new jewelry motifs were created: racing greyhounds and whippets, yachts and boats, and automobiles. Cartoonish stick figures of men and women were colored with enamel, set with rhinestones and pearls, and pinned on hats and handbags as women hunted, fished, golfed, danced, and drank cocktails. Animals were another popular motif for pins, running the range of menagerie inhabitants: parrots, lizards, ducks, birds and bees, as well as cats and dogs.

An absolute first was costume jewelry movie-star memorabilia. Fans could cut out their favorite photos of Mary Pickford or Rudolph Valentino, and snap them into tiny lockets set on a bracelet.

Not all novelties were figurative: initial monograms were among the very first pieces of jewelry and many American jewelry companies got their start manufacturing monogram pieces. The craze was started by the singing and dancing Dolly Sisters, around 1922. Fanatic clotheshorses and trendsetters, the Dollys put their initials on everything in their wardrobe, from hankies to underwear—no small feat. Fashionable followers took up the fancy, and monograms were engraved or set in stones on all types of jewelry, from brooches to stickpins. Monograms were even worn on the feet: monogrammed buckles on shoes, an initialed bracelet around the ankle.

Novelty jewelry also took the form of good-luck symbols, which were available in the best jewelry stores and souvenir shops. Popularized in the gambling dens of the French Riviera, jeweled monkeys, elephants, Chinese coins, and swallows (good luck symbols in France) were dangled by men from their watch fobs. Women put their lucky mascots at the end of a hat pin or strung them on an elephant hair bracelet. Such was fickle fortune that it wasn't unusual to see a cheap costume jewelry lucky piece worn on a priceless diamond bracelet. Lucky jewelry novelties were made of ivory, coral, turquoise, jade, and bone, as well as glass, wood, and composition plastic. From the Riviera the fad spread to the United States, and fashionable women across the country sported lucky charms. (After the stock market crash of 1929, charms were worn with real feeling.)

Couturier Worth created the ultra-modern good-luck mascot in 1928, described by *Style* magazine as " . . . a little 'safety first' fetish to have in the car to ward off accidents. It is a small black figure carved from ebony, with brown suede fringed skirt and cap. A wide leather strap permits this little figure to become an occupant of the car."

BEACH JEWELRY Fashionables of the 1920s dripped with gems even when wet—they bejeweled themselves for the beach. The vogue for suntanning sent women straight to the sand, wearing the craziest swim gear. Women wore tafetta, silk, satin, and crêpe swimsuits, with tiny removable pleated skirts and capes to match. Designed by a master couturier, these suits were just as expensive as an evening gown. This was not surprising, since they used the same fabrics; some of the suits were even detailed with lavish beaded decoration. The stylish beach goer looked like a cross between a mermaid and a ship-wrecked Ziegfeld Follies showgirl.

A witness's description of a beach scene in the south of France in 1928 reads much like a page from *The Great Gatsby*: "The specta-cle of a woman wearing a white satin cos-tume, with full skirt, the skirt sewn with 'diamonds' with a 'diamond' sewn cap, for the sea, is seen . . . while the lady who does not intend to descend into the water wears a striped silk pajama . . . the former is finished with a diamond sautoir, earrings, bracelets, worn in great number, and it is clear that nei-ther costume nor white satin slippers out-lined with 'diamonds,' can bear a wetting."

In the true spirit of the 1920s, it was the impractical that was adored. Necklaces of coral, ivory, lapis, amber, tortoise, mother-of-pearl—and their man-made imitations—were considered appropriate for the beach be-cause they were "natural" materials. Wood was another natural for jewelry: painted or gilded wooden beads were made into hefty chokers and ankle bracelets, often strung on elastic. Thick strands of au naturel shells were slung around the neck, or draped, ban-ner-style, over a bare shoulder. Shells were also used as trim for swimsuits, capes, and straw beach bags.

Costume jewelry for the beach followed strict fashion rules: it was color-coordinated with the rest of the ensemble, made to match the parasol, bathing suit, slippers, or the embroidered silk shawl, cover-up, or cape. Certain colors were considered more suitably "sporty": coral (deep red, salmon, pink), bone and ivory, and black and white.

Rubber jewelry was the smartest of the smart: it was waterproof and very expensive, available at the best department stores. A rubber jewelry parure included a necklace, bangles for the arm, an ankle bracelet, and for the head, a selection of fantastical rubber diving caps, shaped like helmets, draped turbans, chef's toques, or fish-scaled mer-maid caps, all garnished with rubber fruit, flowers, and frills. Rubberized satin ker-chiefs were also knotted around the head

No stylish bather's get-up was complete without a rubber toy. Rubber penguins, modeled after Charles Lindbergh's good luck mascot, were a favorite. The most fashionble pet was a rubber duckie, worn clutched un-der the bather's arm.

CIGARETTE RINGS Of course women smoked, and the long, rhinestone-studded cigarette holder is a familiar piece of equip-ment. What's not as known is the cigarette ring. The dainty smoker had feminine "gas-pers," baby-sized cigarettes—just enough for a few puffs between dances. The cigarettes were held by a finger ring; women could smoke without touching a cigarette (but lift-ing a finger).

SHOE JEWELS Women had rings on their fingers and jewels on the toes of their shoes. Shop girls and society gals alike added sparkle to their Cinderella evening slippers. Of course, the rich kicked up their heels with the real thing: one celebrated socialite set her initials—in genuine diamonds—into the heels of her shoes. Mrs. Florenz Ziegfeld (of the Ziegfeld Follies) studded her bedroom slippers with sapphires.

But even the working girl could wear slippers made of gold or silver kidskin, satin, brocade, or silk, covered with glass beads or sequins. Shoe straps were solid rhinestones or pearls. The heel was glorious, inlaid with rhinestones, mother-of-pearl, bits of mirror, ebony, glass crystals, steel beads, or pearls. How these spectacular shoes were rejeweled after a frantic night of dancing the Charleston is a mystery.

Anything in a lady's wardrobe could take to jewelry-like ornament. This handbag has a fancy metal clasp, boasting the same trimmings found on jewelry.

Vanity cases held lipstick, powder, perfume, and occasionally playing cards. This model, made by Napier, was worn bracelet-style, suspended from a cord around the wrist.

Everything in Sport Jewelry

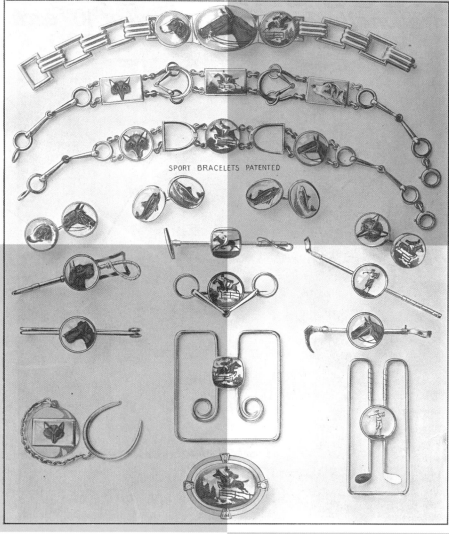

SPORT BRACELETS PATENTED

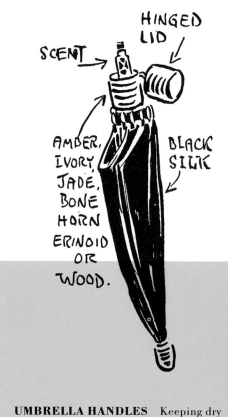

SCENT → HINGED LID ↙

AMBER, IVORY, JADE, BONE HORN ERINOID OR WOOD.

BLACK SILK ↙

A 1928 sample of sports jewelry for the fashionable man who hunted, golfed, or rode horses. These items were made of glass pieces set in metal, and painted on the back side of the glass.

UMBRELLA HANDLES Keeping dry was done in high style, as the humble umbrella was transformed from functional to fashionable. The well-dressed woman was distinguished by the fact that her umbrella's silk cover matched her silk dress, and that her bracelets matched the umbrella's handle. Like costume jewelry, the umbrellas' handles were of real and imitation ebony, bone, gold and silver, gilt woods, horn, and amber. Umbrellas were also handled with a menagerie of cartoon characters lifted straight from novelty jewelry: the identical carved ducks, parrots, birds, dogs, and penguins found on brooches and bracelets.

One of the signatures of the 1920s was its love of amusing little gadgets: cigarette lighters, vanity cases, portable cocktail sets. Multi-purpose accessories were considered especially "amusing" and "modern." For example, unscrew an umbrella handle—voila! Out popped a tiny bottle of perfume. Cigarettes, lipstick, or a flask of bootleg liquor could also be stashed in that secret hollow handle.

Necklet Fastenings.—top: Tubular and (below) Barrel Snap, with V-spring; Box Snap and Spring; threaded Screw; bottom: hollow Bolt-Ring; Toggle Bar and Ring; Swivel; Diamond or Paste-set Snap (Fig. 65).

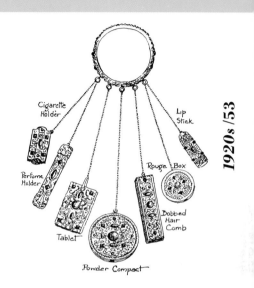

CHATELAINE UPDATE The moderns updated the chatelaine, relic of the Victorian age. This 1920s version had a treasure trove of can't-be-without items hooked to tiny chains on a ring or bracelet.

SHOULDER FLOWERS The flapper was never without her jewels—or a flower on her shoulder. The corsage flower was always worn pinned on the left shoulder or at the waist, and the blooms could be real or artificial. Certain types of flowers were worn with certain types of dress: field flowers such as daisies and violets were for morning and afternoon wear; while huge peonies, poppies, roses, and pompons—fantasies made up in metallic cloth, lacquered silk, feathers, tulle, kid, and patent leather—were de rigueur in the evening. Jeweled with dew that didn't come from Mother Nature, the petals of these blooms were sprinkled with rhinestones, beads, and fake pearls.

Around 1927, clothing styles changed, and accessories did, too. The shoulder corsage flower fell from favor and was replaced by the shoulder brooch, buckle, and slightly later, the pair of clip brooches, all better suited for holding up the new-fashioned dresses, which featured shoulder-draped panels, gathers, and tiers.

The slightly risqué ankle bracelet enjoyed a wave of popularity among naughty flappers.

30's

The stylish look of the 1930s was a curious blend of flouncing femininity, streamlined modernity, and humor. One explanation: ". . . the backwards turn of feminine fashion, which—whatever it may do tomorrow—has successfully confused the very old with the very new and somehow made the result perfectly congruous. Consequently poke bonnets are today obscuring from view the lofty heights of the Chrysler Building, evening trains sweep elegantly over the mirrored floors of the jazziest night clubs, and pinched-in waistlines are being exhibited by the very best young ladies on the tennis court and golf green." One style didn't supersede another, and a jumble of fashions coexisted. "We have come to the River of Doubt in fashion," sighed the *Pictorial Review* magazine, suffering from the too-many-choices syndrome. "What to wear?" must have been a glorious—and bewildering—question. Costume jewelry offered equally multiple styles—the chief hallmarks were a very theatrical glamour and a surrealistic humor.

The 1930s woman was smart, chic, swank. Photographer Cecil Beaton, who had his eye on the American female, wrote, "You will see the typical New York Venus tottering down Park Avenue, with pallid, poreless, kid-glove skin; large mouth, flamboyantly painted; hard, bright eyelets; well-constructed jaw; high cheekbones; and flowing mane of hair. She wears the uniform of neat skin-tight black dress, fresh little cutlet frills at collar and cuffs, a row of pearls, loosely hanging mink coat, excessively well-cut new shoes and a mad hat (with perhaps half a bird on it)."

A close-up of Venus could be startling. *Mademoiselle* described beauties circa 1937: "Their make-up is theatrical, with a marked preference for thick, moist lipstick. They either wear false eyelashes or else mascara their own so heavily that they look false." The 1930s fashionable woman prided herself on how divorced she was from the flapper of just a few years, or seasons, ago. The flapper languished, relegated to the "old-fashioned" corner. Apparently, her banishment was welcome. Mooed a fashion magazine, "Men . . . welcome again the swish of a long skirt, the twinkling of eyes behind a veil . . . along with the new feminine mannerisms." Attitude, manners, fashion changed. The *Junior League* magazine indicated the telling metamorphosis from the all-bones flapper into the 1930s stylish debutante: "Nina, Marion, and their crowd eat more

A Rococo take-off (opposite page): an elaborate glass and pearl pendant worn on a ribbon. Whimsical ear of corn brooch (above) boasts invisibly set cut stones and enamel.

than they would have a few years ago. When you go to their parties you are apt to hear, 'Please pass the rolls,' and 'Yes, thank you, a little more chicken.' " What a switch from the flapper who was likely to stub out her cigarette on her salad plate, never mind saying "please" or cleaning her plate. Her 1930s-era replacements were the bold babe in a man-tailored, sharp-angled suit who could "wolf a man"; Hollywood's languid glamor girl; the madcap dame who screamed "you're a howl"; and the debutante.

They lived in feverish times. Starting with the 1929 stock market crash's ruined millionaires, the Depression pinched pockets and jewelry boxes; for the first few years of the 1930s fine jewelry and lavish couture costume pieces went into hiding. Even Cecil Beaton was moved to write, "It is vulgar to be rich and extravagant . . . even if you haven't lost money, you must pretend you have." Then, when gold was taken out of circulation in 1933, it prompted a gold rush; precious and costume jewelry became bigger, bolder, golder than ever.

While the Depression-era socialite could still be counted on to support the occasional gold bracelet and the riches of Paris couture, loyalties underwent a subtle shift. French couture was still in first place, but now American-made creations were competitors—not just copies. Musical comedies and period films offered heavenly escape to the Depression-weary. The movies were also one of the best vehicles for fashion's display. Motion-picture studios had a galaxy of native American talent designing costumes and costume jewelry for the movies, and their work was quickly knocked off for the mass market. California was a fresh source of inspiration, and for a time "Made in Hollywood" or "Made in California" on a clothing label had the same magic as "Made in Paris." And American nightlife offered places to show it all—café society haunts like the Stork Club and El Morocco, filled with the music of Cole Porter and the big bands.

Stars like Marlene Dietrich, Greta Garbo, and Joan Crawford were among the fashion idols of the period. When Garbo and Katharine Hepburn wore tailored pants, so did millions of American women. Real-life wardrobes reflected the variety of costume drama dressing that Hollywood dished up. *Style Arts* compared 1930s fashion to the song, "Anything Goes." Choosing what to wear, they wrote, " . . . may well confuse a genius unless she dusts off her books on costume history and does a little boning up between buying trips."

Versatile as an actress, the 1930s woman tossed on one style after another, following fashion's parade through history. Her choices included an imitation of a turn-of-the-century belle or France's Empress Eugénie. The all-out glamour of the Hollywood look suited her, as did California-inspired play togs and the witty

Harper's Bazaar *featured this couturier costume jewelry in 1939 (top to bottom): Molyneux pear-and-leaf brooch; Schiaparelli white-bear ornament fastened with a chain; a a tiny figure with a watch for a head and a spring for a body, by Boinet; varanished real walnuts set with fabric leaves to make a brooch, by Molyneux.*

garb inspired by a funky surrealism—with a dose of Walt Disney thrown in. With each season, and with each of these fashion masquerades, there was costume jewelry.

Costume jewelry claimed its own turf in this hectic decade. Unabashedly fake, these baubles were ready for showtime, in larger-than-life size. Simple streamlined bracelets smothered the wrist. Necklaces continued to borrow barbaric and exotic inspiration—primarily from India. Rococo clips held up the flimsy drapery of the new clinging gowns. Shiny gold and shameless rhinestones were the favored ingredients. Humor became a force to recognize: surrealism and its high priestess, Elsa Schiaparelli of Paris, practiced sorcery with fashion and jewelry, transforming an array of insects, animals, and odd objects into costume pieces.

The 1930s jewelry industry experienced a mighty boom. Improved mass production was able to turn out jewelry in volume, and improved technology made the recent new synthetic—plastic—more versatile than ever. The range of other materials and jewelry-making techniques expanded, too, inaugurating the use of novel combinations of materials on a single piece of jewelry.

Toward the end of the decade, war in Europe began to affect the fashion and costume jewelry industries in the United States. The rumble of war had been in the air for some time; in 1936 *Harper's Bazaar* had reviewed a new dress style with the sharp comment, "Directoire—or shall we call it dictatoire?" In August 1939 the French fashion industry ground to a halt. Early in 1939 jewelry imports from Czechoslovakia—a major source for stones and beads—were curtailed, and American jewelry companies began to stockpile materials. France was still able to export materials but was unable to meet the American jewelry industry demand. As Europe slid into World War II, America was pretty much on its own. Materials were scarce, and there was no fashion leadership from the Parisian couture houses or the fine jewelers. Consumers did not notice any dramatic style lapses or shortages until 1940; by that time manufacturers had used up their back stock, and it was time to improvise.

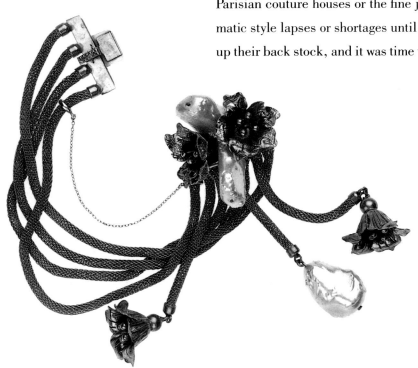

Gold mesh bracelet (left) with baroque pearls by Schiaparelli.

ROMANCE RETURNS

Who would have thought the streamlined 1930s would backlash into hearts and flowers? "Women are going weaker sex with a vengeance," swore *Vogue* in 1935. The *Junior League* magazine gave the reason: "We have our depressing responsibilities during the day; in the evening we need contrast, softness, leisure."

Victorian Revival

As early as 1931, and continuing through the end of the decade, Victorian motifs were the sweet and sentimental favorites of the ladies. The flapper's crazy fashions of the 1920s had nosedived. Women fell for ostrich-feather trimmings, flounces, ruffles, jet and sequin embroidery. Couturiers offered leg-o'-mutton sleeves, capes and capelets, bustles, and peplums. Nosegays of violets were brandished. Gloves had sixteen buttons. Snoods made a comeback. At night, skirts fell to the anklebone.

Women didn't completely fall for Victorian dressing; they were selective, adopting its trimmings (the ruffles and peplums) and especially its accessories (hats, handbags, gloves, costume jewelry). It was the Victorian "spirit" fashion was after, not a replica.

The honor for the popular revival of Victoriana was laid at the feet of film stars, notably Mae West. Her 1933 film *She Done Him Wrong*, set in the Victorian era, sent couturiers swooning. "Evening clothes are strangely glamorous—and the inspiration of this elusive quality is strangely enough our own Mae West . . . the couturiers were among Miss West's most rabid fans. Her gowns—rich, vital, and heartily elegant like her personality—entranced them. Almost every designer came out with at least one evening gown traceable to the West-ian influence," pointed out *Style* magazine in 1934. In Paris (where the film was titled Lady Lou), Mae West worship grew so acute that there were even parties in her honor. *Vogue*

Cameos were borrowed from the Victorians: here, a plastic cameo in an antique-looking metal setting.

Victorian revival: Victorian-style link metal bracelets embellished with charms (right and opposite page). Hat pins made a comeback, and Schiaparelli made this ornate model (top) and the hat pin shaped like a knife handle next to it.

was there: "Mrs. Trefusis' party at the Tour Eiffel, where smart women came as Mae West, marked a date in fashion history."

In addition to Mae West, plenty of other silver-screen stars invigorated the romantic trend, including Bette Davis as the Empress Carlotta in *Juarez* (set in the 1860s) and Claudette Colbert in *Zaza* (set at the turn of the century). Both *Juarez* and the later *Gone With the Wind* sparked their own lines of licensed costume jewelry.

Costume jewelry of the 1930s materials aped those used by the Victorians: "jet" (black glass or plastic), tiny pearls, marcasite, bits of coral, turquoise, moonstone, garnet, and amethyst. Victoriana also incorporated engraving and lacy gold-and-silver filigree, sugared with cupids, fruit, flowers, and leaves. The charm bracelet, the chatelaine brooch, and the cameo were reeditioned, as were dog collars and chokers. There were pendants and lockets on large chains and crosses too big to be pious. All of this, yelped the *National Jeweler*, "verged on the border of fussiness." Some costume jewelry was an exact, line-for-line copy of antique Victorian pieces. Other jewelry attempted to re-create its image without much historical accuracy, so that *Women's Wear Daily* could state, "The early 1900s spirit. . . may also be responsible for the renewal of black in jewelry."

What's most interesting about this Victorian revival was how the clunky sensibility of the 1930s, married to the new materials, twisted the style in its own way. The unlikely and the delightful happened: the cameo mutated into a jokey giant made up in definitely non–nineteenth-century colors like crayon green, blue, and chrome yellow, dangling from an oversized chain. Thanks to modern technology, that plastic cameo could also be gold-plated. Massive hinged bracelets were painted with delicate Victorian posies, which would have made genuine Victorians shudder. With its close-to-kitsch attitude, this jewelry had a hybrid vigor, a happy blend of the Victorian and novelty styles.

Victorian-look pearl choker pictured in a 1939 Bergdorf Goodman ad.

Rococo Revisited

The romantic ghost of the French Empress Eugénie was an ever more palpable presence in 1930s fashion. *Style* magazine decreed that Eugénie "need no longer squirm in her final resting place," since she hadn't been forgotten. Women craved what the empress represented: true femininity. The Rococo style associated with Empress Eugénie (or "E. E.," as she was familiarly called) was an aspect of the 1930s cult of feminine romance. This cult was home to the Rococo and the Victorian fashion revivals, which overlapped and were sometimes confused, with their fussy signature frills and frippery. Bare, draped necklines, veils, lace-mitt gloves, and feather trimmings were all rather vaguely associated with Eugénie's Second Empire era. The Eugénie hat was a direct crib—a tiny plumed affair, worn confidently cocked forward on the head. More than just a quaint revival, it was a major fashion fad, launched in 1931.

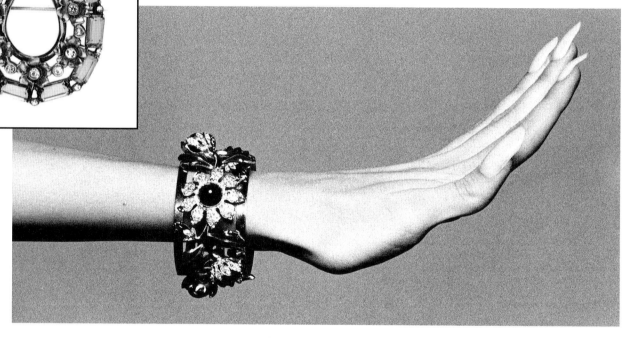

Rococo-revival jewelry mirrored these styles, turning out elaborate, dainty pieces with a ladylike scale. Originally, Eugénie's jewelry had been the love token offerings of Napoleon III, emperor of France. Eugénie herself had a special fondness for Marie Antoinette, her predecessor, and in her honor, Eugénie adopted a few of her signature motifs. In the 1930s the jewelry associated with Eugénie was a rich mix of motifs, some Rococo. Among the most prevalent motifs was the ribbon, which was furled and unfurled into streamers, curves, and bowknots. Other favorites included the tassel, the garland, laurel leaves, scallop shells, cherubs, feathers, wings, the royal crown, and a pair of lovebirds.

These motifs appear again and again in costume jewelry, created in a variety of materials. Gold was the precious metal of royalty; "antique" gold was considered an especially authentic reproduction. The scrolling motifs were also traced in white metal set with all rhinestones or with rhinestones mixed with one other kind of gemstone—rubies, emeralds, or sapphires. The mix of rubies and rhinestones was an important 1930s combination—the signal accompaniment to the all-white evening dress.

Two elaborate pins by Eisenberg: sterling silver set with pink, cut stones, and a horseshoe of topaz stones (top); Enamel and pavé stone gold metal bracelet by Coro (right); Chanel's real diamonds as they were displayed on lifelike wax mannequins (opposite page) for her jewelry collection in 1932. Pearl and amethyst colored stone girandole earrings (top, far right) by Joseff of Hollywood.

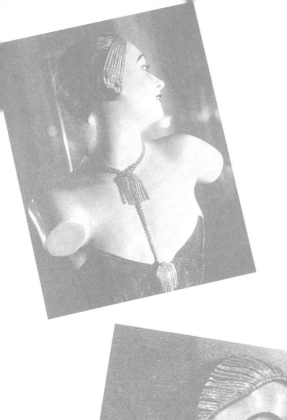

Rococo jewelry in the 1930s was more sculptural, more three-dimensional than its earlier, less significant incarnation in the 1920s. The jewelry had a "punched-out" look, created by the strong negative spaces between the tracery of the lines in the design. Although this jewelry used swirls and flourishes, echoing the shaped elegance of the typical 1930s dress with its bias-cut drapery, it also had an underlying current of angular geometry.

As a style, the Rococo was associated with royalty, and the most prominent royal emblem was the crown. One of the most widely popular motifs, the crown—a bow to the cornonation of George VI as King of England in 1936—came in all sizes, shapes, and materials, with or without jewels, to decorate lapels, necks, and ears.

Even Schiaparelli used elements of the Rococo. In 1934 her costume jewelry offering was a gold metal brooch of arrows and wings; in 1938 she put chubby little cherubs on brooches, clips, and earrings.

Chanel played with Rococo designs, too, and her 1932 jewelry collection set a trend that ran for the rest of the decade. The astringent simplicity of her 1920s jewelry was elaborated, its new look attributed to her collaboration with the jewelry designer the Duke of Verdura. Their dazzling jewelry was made with real diamonds and platinum—unexpected from a woman who had trumpeted costume jewelry. Although these lavish pieces were acidly criticized as "vulgar," Chanel was shrewd enough to anticipate that this was jewelry made to be copied, not sold. As *Vogue*'s review pointed out, this diamond loot would give women the courage to wear rhinestones that looked just like precious stones. Costume jewelry pricked up its stylish ears and picked up her motifs, elements of a Rococo/Baroque sensibility. These included the five-, six-, and seven-pointed star, stars mounted on half-moon crescents or stars trailing a comet tail, sole crescents, arrows, comets, enormous sunbursts, slender crosses, and bowknots. Several of Chanel's necklaces sported tassels; a curled feather became a brooch and a tiara; and a sheaf of diamond wheat was a hair ornament.

When they were originally shown, Chanel's diamonds were draped on life-like wax busts exhibited in her private home. Her display innovation—clamping the diamond clips on the mannequin's fur cape—was widely copied, in both costume and fine jewelry. It was a good reason to move jewelry up a notch to a bigger scale; clips and brooches grew mammoth, herculean, for the task of adorning bulky fur collars, capes, and coats.

Pearls and Beads

Pastel-tinted pearls were part of the romantic trend of the early 1930s. The fashion got its start in the late 1920s with the "suntan" pearl, but by 1939 the range of colors included those of Elsa Schiaparelli's line—smoke, light amethyst, flower green, and nosegay (light blue)—created for D. Lisner in New York. Pink and baby blue pearls and beads were the chic costume jewelry choices (as were their genuine counterparts, coral and turquoise). Internationally known decorator and socialite Elsie de Wolfe may have set the trend—the ultra-fashionable pearl, like Elsie's hair, was dyed pale blue. Pastels were also the most becoming colors for the 1930s femme fatale, the blonde bombshell. "Sky blue and aquamarine blue are the 1930s gift to the blue-eyed blonde," cooed the *National Jeweler*. Pastel jewelry also accompanied fashion's new turn: the white dress. White replaced black as the color of choice for evening wear during the early 1930s, interpreted in clingy satin and crêpe. Couturier Vionnet's draped, Grecian-style gowns epitomized the

Triple tiers of pearls or white glass beads make up a classic 1930s necklace.

slinky look and the hushed palette. Even legs were pale, clad in pastel maize, pink, and blue stockings, described by *Pictorial Review* in 1930 as "scarcely more than a dusting of powder over the legs." Those powder-pale legs were quite a switch from the sunburned, nut-brown legs of the flapper.

Originally, light-colored jewelry was only for resort wear or for wearing with spring and summer's flowered chiffons. However, when "the little black dress" became a daytime standard by the end of the 1920s, pale pearls and beads became its most popular accessories. White pearls massed at throat and wrist were encouraged by a Chanel dress of the mid-1930s: a black dress with her signature collar and cuffs. "Black, as usual, is predominating at the Ritz during the tea hour," reported *Style* magazine in 1935. "Sometimes a short, triple, or even quadruple-strand pearl necklace relieves the somewhat trying effect of the high black neckline." Smooth glass beads in opaque polar-bear white were a new innovation, and they were made into the same types of jewelry as their pearl cousins.

Beads and pearls of the 1930s weren't in the load-'em-on, down-to-the-knees style of the 1920s—these were real ladies. Neatly elegant, they were worn in tidy double- and triple-strand necklaces and matching bracelets; braided chokers were also favorites. One fine distinction between the 1920s and the 1930s necklace was the latter's asymmetrical arrangement. The necklace clasp, or a single ornament, was moved to the front of the necklace, creating a "lopsided" effect.

The resurrection of another necklace style—the pearl dog collar—brought the Victorians back onto the pearl scene. The collar hadn't changed much since the days of Queen Victoria: it was secured with a fancy, stone-studded clasp or strung on flexible wire to slip around the neck. The revival of the pearl dog collar can be traced to the rash of Victorian period-style films: *Lillian Russell*, *The Barretts of Wimpole Street*, and *Saratoga Trunk*. The ribbon-and-pearl necklace was another charming novelty linked with the Victorians: a velvet ribbon was knotted to half a string of pearls and tied in a bow at the back of the neck.

CHANEL Credited with propelling women's fashion into the twentieth century, Coco Chanel is almost as famous for her costume jewelry as she is for her clothing. She was born in 1883 in Auverge and opened a dressmaking shop in Paris in 1914. Her jewelry designs began with simple rhinestones in the 1920s, moving on to diamonds in the early 1930s. The jewelry recognizable as "Chanel" is a 1950s development; its materials and motifs were adapted from Renaissance pieces. According to Diana Vreeland, Chanel's fake pearls were copies of the fabulous Romanov pearls given to her by her lover the Grand Duke Dimitri of Russia. Madame Gripoix, of Gripoix Jewelry in Paris, has made most of Chanel's costume jewelry since the 1930s. She recalls that Chanel carried her own priceless jewelry in a paper bag and would spill it out on the floor of her office. Customarily, Chanel sprawled on the carpet to work, copying the valuable originals in soft wax to make costume duplicates. Chanel's jewelry has changed little since the 1950s. She died in 1971.

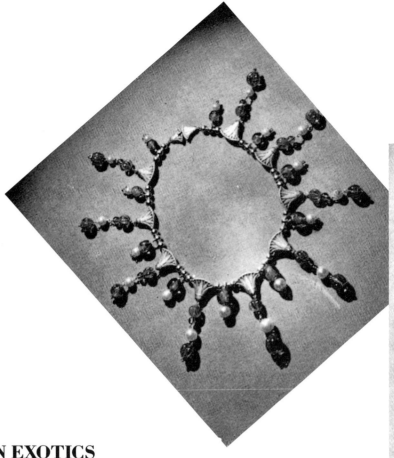

EASTERN EXOTICS

"Strange and exotic shapes! Strange and glorious colors! Pins for your modern dress like those that fasten scarves. Bangly bracelets for your arm that might dangle by the dozen on the arm of a Hindu princess." These were the seductive words of a 1935 fashion ad describing the appeal of "East Indian"- or "Eastern Oriental"-style costume jewelry, one of the decade's recurrent motifs.

"Indian" jewelry was bold and eye-catching and had fashion writers gushing reverently that it was "massive" and "important." "Insignificance is the only sin," preached *Vogue* in 1938. Hardly insignificant, necklaces were hung in a V-shape from throat to waist like a big bib or golden chest armor. And they made noise, clanking and jangling with coins, beads, spikes, spears, balls, and rocks, made up in wood, plastic, or glass. Gemstones for these necklaces looked like the real thing—fake amber, amethyst, turquoise, onyx, coral, and imitation pearls, rubies, and emeralds. The stones of choice were rough and worn, rather than neatly cut and polished dazzlers. In spite of its bristly appearance, this jewelry was predominantly flat and flexible, rather than stiffly rigid or protruding.

The bib necklace came in a dizzying variety of draped and cascading chains, latticework plastrons, and metal ropes shaking with beads, balls, bells, and a treasure-chest assortment of very faux gems. Sometimes all of these ingredients were combined in a single necklace. A variation was the necklace of metal chain or fringe looped into the classic bib shape. Bracelets—flexible, flat mesh bands or heavily beaded versions—were as oversized as the necklaces they matched. Earrings were rarely made to match the necklace and bracelet set and were typically bunchy hanging drops or grapelike clusters of beads or coins.

As shown in Harper's Bazaar *in 1939: Chanel's gold necklace of green and pink stones and pearls (top left) and a blue-bead necklace with a blue cord tie (top right). Topaz-bead and gold-metal necklace (bottom) by Chanel fastens with a silk cord in back.*

Chanel (opposite page), photographed by Horst.

Actress Beatrice Lillie (top) in an elaborate
Oriental bib necklace. Gold-metal and glass-
bead necklace (bottom) by Napier.

What earmarks East Indian jewelry as pure 1930s style is its material—gold metal—and its weighty look. Its exotic aura and humor, made it well received by the fashion hounds. In spite of its disorderly appearance, the loopy luxe of its cascades and drapes, the jewelry had a slightly "tailored" feeling; the pieces were always symmetrical.

The bib necklace, with all its ornamentation in front, was related to the "Hawaiian lei" flower necklaces of the late 1920s and early 1930s. The East Indian bib took the same bulky necklace structure, substituted metal and beads for the flowers, and flattened the whole thing out. Besides the overscale bib, the Indian style was also translated into a dog collar fringed with a long row of beads. Yet another variation was the collar necklace, with an identical front and back, which could be worn either way. Clasps for all these necklaces were a minor detail, nearly indistinguishable from the necklace itself; some bibs were strung on silk cord or ribbon and tied at the back of the neck.

A sidekick to East Indian jewelry became a classic: Chanel in 1939 (and simultaneously, Paquin) introduced coin necklaces: round gold disks dangling from a long chain. These were called "gypsy" necklaces. Four years earlier, coins were already clinking on clips and necklaces, a spin-off from charm bracelets. The classic chain, strung with semi-precious colored gemstone beads and pearls, was also worn with the gypsy and Indian bib necklaces.

the lady: Fili-
necklace, **18.79**
her birds, **1.83**

A famous woman's
East Indian neck-
lace, copied in simu-
lated stones __**7.44**

The taste for Eastern exotica was kick-started by current events, including a series of international fairs and expositions, including the Colonial Exhibition of 1931, the so-called French Exposition of 1937 (both held in Paris), and the New York World's Fair of 1939. Another stellar event kept the passion for India going: the king of England was crowned emperor of India in 1937. The expositions also brought the arts and culture of Morocco, Algeria, Java, Malaysia, and Cambodia into the spotlight, and these countries were cheerfully plundered for fashion inspiration. "The natives of Algeria little knew that in designing the bold and colorful jewelry of their native land that the effect of those designs would be felt in the . . . jewelry for the smart set of the metropolitan centers," yapped a New York store ad in 1930. For costume jewelry, the labels "Indian," "Algerian," and "Moroccan" were indiscriminately used, and pretty much interchangeable.

Fashion took the exotic look further, directly stealing styles from the native costumes of India and Turkey, calling the gowns "Hindu" dresses. In the spring of 1935 couturier Mainbocher did Turkish skirts, and Alix did gold-bordered gauze scarves, worn with sandals flat as a dervish dancer's. Schiaparelli's couture collection was on the "Hindu" bandwagon, too, and *Vogue* was there to report. "What completely stunned the Western world were draped Hindu dresses. Into Schiap's Place Vendôme house, all festivity, flowers, and champagne for the opening, drifted mannequins looking like Hindu princesses. Saris or harem scarves were draped over their heads."

Of course, a woman didn't need to dress like a Hindu princess to carry off the Indian-style jewelry. The flexibility of the jewelry was perfectly suited to the dress that was the 1930s standard: it was either collarless or had a high neck; the front bodice was bare of trimming and showed off to advantage the flat spread of the big bib necklace. That dress was usually black, a good match with gold jewelry. It was a match that lasted throughout the entire decade. Said a Bonwit Teller store advertisement of 1933, ". . . all of the Paris couturiers . . . made such grand gold jewelry that they are to a great degree responsible for this fashion of black and gold." The black dress could show off gold bracelets as well, with sleeves that were long and slim or short, so that those massive clincher cuff bracelets went right to the wrist. Fantasy was the selling point, ready to transport the wearer from her simple black dress to something more alluring: "These are the dancing girl bracelets of Morocco. Wear them in pairs as the dancing girls do. They'll remind you of vivid scenes and costumes of North Africa. . . . "

Jewelry

Jewelry

PUT it on, PILE it on

THE NEW BARBARIANS

The taste for jewelry that was big, bad, and barbaric was given a new push from the 1931 Colonial Exhibition in France. All of fashionable Paris crowded to see the art and artifacts gathered from French colonies around the world. The hoopla surrounding the exhibition inspired a taste for new exotica, and Asia and North Africa were its sources. Even Folies dancer Josephine Baker's famous banana-skirt costume changed with the times: the bananas were replaced by tusks in 1932.

Costume jewelry took a lesson from the thrilling bracelets and necklaces on display—made of real animal teeth and claws. Even in the midst of the advances of the machine-inspired Moderne style, Mother Nature held her own. A good part of barbaric jewelry's appeal was in this contrast: its savagery and its huge scale emphasized a woman's frailty and femininity. *Vogue* took up the attitude, predicting the jewelry forecast for fall of 1933, "bulk and more bulk seems to be the cry of the moment."

This bulky jewelry was translated into many different materials. The barbaric, 1930s style, was made of the same rough stuff seen in the 1920s: wood, cork, bone, shells, leather. However, now plastic was more predominant; newly versatile, it became the perfect material for super-scaled jewelry, since it could be oversized without being overweight. Slightly more polished than the cork-on-a-string-type necklaces of the 1920s, barbaric jewelry the second time around was occasionally trimmed with suitably rough ornaments: nailhead studs, primitive carving, large rough stones. Color turned gayer, too, especially in the plastic pieces.

The jewelry's bold swagger and size rank it as truly barbaric. A row of massive egg-sized beads, plain or savagely carved, made a barbaric necklace. Bracelets were huge, heavy-looking wrist swallowers, spectacularly awkward and a little dangerous to wear. The *National Jeweler* honed in on such a bracelet, describing it as " . . . carved from a single piece of stone." It credited Parisian couturier Louiseboulanger with showing it first in the spring of 1930. Her other model was a bracelet that was "a solid piece of composition in enormous size, open at one side to slip over the wrist." Another bracelet novelty of this time was the two-piece bracelet made with a hinge similar to the one used on the clip brooch. The sectioned cuff bracelet also got the fashionable nod: thick, chunky slabs of plastic or wood were strung together on thin elastic. The "ruff" section bracelet was a variation, made to flare out around the wrist, "inspired seemingly by the paper frill on a hambone," noted one wit.

Big and barbaric: a Bakelite bracelet (top) strung on elastic. Just as hefty: a hand-carved plastic bracelet (bottom), three inches wide.

Most barbaric jewelry looked as if it were made by hall-of-the-mountain-king trolls. A flowery variation, which could have been made by Snow White and her helpers, was more delicate. While theme and materials were different for both these types, the effect was the same—the jewelry projected a massive quality. The more fragile version was composed of tiny elements—berrylike beads, flowers, petals, drops, and leaf shapes—in glass, transparent plastic, porcelain, crystal, semi-precious stones, and enameled metals strung on a flexible base. Prickly coral was also a favorite material. Strands of these tiny elements would be twisted, twined, and braided together to create bulky, untamed jewelry. Set around wrist or throat, it looked more like a jungle shrub than a graceful bouquet. It was noisy, too. Jewelry thick with "petals, leaves, spikes, or just with huge sugar-lump and moth-ball beads" jangled and jiggled when it moved. A flower necklace was called "Rustle of Spring" because of the melody of its glass morning glories knocking together.

Fashion copy of the day called these jewels "Hawaiian lei" necklaces. The style can be traced back to couturier Norman Hartnell, who showed the original glass lei necklace in Paris in 1929. Another source was the multiple-strand bead and seed-pearl necklaces popular at the same time. A tropical influence also drifted in from movies like *Typhoon* and *Lady of the Tropics*. Actress Dorothy Lamour was famous for her sarong, and her flower accessories were watched closely, too.

Like the vrai lei, some of the necklaces had flowers all around; other ornamentation was centered toward the front. Bracelets were also trimmed the same way; describing a clear plastic bead bracelet, a fashion writer flattered that it looked "like hundreds of crystalline bubbles attached to the wrist." In another variation, several strands of beads held a flower-edged medallion on the wrist. Even clip brooches followed the lei style.

Colored wood-bead necklace (top) from the late 1930s by Miriam Haskell; in the boxes (right and bottom): plastic and glass-bead bracelets and a clip, heavy with ornament.

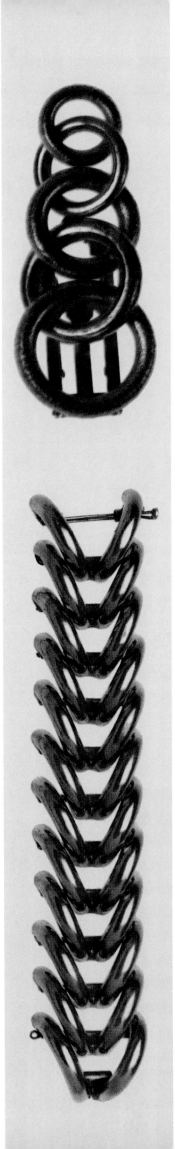

STREAMLINED MODERN

The 1930s had its own rah-rah attitude about being the "modern age." Speed and urgency were part of it, what was called the "don't write—telegraph mood of the present day." Living in the modern age also meant embracing the revolutionary new aesthetics of industry: machine design. Machine design wasn't restricted to just airplane engines, it touched on every aspect of life. "Design," explained *Arts and Decoration* magazine, "is affecting our daily bread, our comfort, our efficiency, our emotions and our nerves." Every object could be improved, streamlined, made more beautiful, more modern. Towering new skyscrapers (such as the Empire State Building) were familiar symbols of the modern age. "A machine for living" was the architect Le Corbusier's cold-blooded definition of the home. Even Noel Coward picked up on the modern mode, titling one of his plays *Design for Living*.

Machine design sought nothing less than the redefinition of beauty. "It has at last dawned on us . . . that the beauty of the twentieth century will be a form molded by the machine, and therefore unlike the ideal of any other age," an art magazine editorialized in 1934. Superstar industrial designers such as Norman Bel Geddes, Gilbert Rohde, and Russel Wright bestowed twentieth-century beauty on objects from pianos to thermometers, radios, dishes, watches, stoves, and business machines.

Schiaparelli strings polished pistons and fretted metal balls on her latest vagary. Characteristically original, and undeniably handsome, smart women will recognize it to be a stimulant to their spirits and their new short sleeved frocks.

Opposite page: a clip (top) and a linked chain-metal bracelet (bottom), both gold metal. Schiaparelli's bulky bracelet studded with blue stones (right) on front and back. Massive necklaces of hollow gold-metal beads (bottom) by Napier.

It's uncertain whether any of these illustrious designers had a hand in designing costume jewelry. They certainly were influential, because in its own way, jewelry followed their principles of good machine design: it had an impersonal look, and a simple surface was favored over detail, ornament, or texture. When there was decoration, it was minimal, a line or indentation—no messy squiggles, elaborate trim, or sparkly bits. Stones, mainly bulky, dull cabochons, were used sparingly. Surfaces were broken up into sculpted planes, creating a rich, 3-D play of light and shadow.

In the 1920s modern jewelry had Art Deco characteristics and a thin, sharp, brittle appearance. The modern jewelry of the 1930s shared the abstraction of the 1920s work, but its streamlining and generous scale gave it a more fluid look. Like the 1920s designs, 1930s jewelry lifted shapes from machinery, but the latter let those shapes relax, made them a little less shrill.

Clips, bracelets, brooches, and necklaces all looked like fragments from a car fender or a toaster. Even the manufacturers' names for this jewelry promised modernity: there were "streamline" clips and "airflow" bracelets. The Napier Company's 1934 jewelry collection was called "machine age." Modern-style jewelry was anti-fuss, anti-ornament, anti-romance. Its fashionable appeal was wonderfully put in a B. Altman's advertisement in 1932, "Spring's a different girl this year! No hearts and flowers—no sweeping draperies—no stealing in on silver-slippered feet! Instead she's marching—swinging—swaggering in—with a sharp, clean, TAILORED silhouette—." Angular, severe suits, and the black daytime dress—with a round, unadorned collar—were the perfect background for modern jewelry.

In the middle of the Depression, nothing cheered like the three G's: glitter, glamor, and gold. Gold was the material of the modern—gold and its imitations in pink, white, and green metals, and in silver, copper, and sometimes aluminum. Surface finishes were mat or shiny. Gold made up for the simplicity of the modern style. It was strong, rich, and hard to miss. Another reason for its popular prominence in costume jewelry was rooted in a real-life, real-gold event. President Roosevelt took gold out of circulation in 1933, stirring up a craving for metal—or even just an imitation of it.

Conspicuous flash was the idea, and gold jewelry grew massive. "Big and clattering" were the adjectives used to describe costume jewelry's incredible hulks. Multiple-strand metal pieces took up plenty of neck room. Bracelets became so big they could only be worn over gloves or over sleeves; neither gloves nor sleeves could fit over them. Gold clips on coats, furs, hats, and scarves were a can't-be-missed four or five inches across.

Gold metal-bead necklaces were what the 1930s modern girl wore instead of pearls. Golden beads and balls came all in one size, or in a graduated assortment. Machine-inspired hollow tubes, oblongs, and pipe-shaped beads were also part of the vocabulary. These gleaming beads mimicked the classical pearl necklace format in single, double, even triple strands. Chokers were also a fa-

vorite length, worn nestled closely about the throat. The modern look included chains—big, overscaled links, or tight snake chains, in the same format of single or multiple strands. Simple earrings and a bulky link of flexible beads or mesh for the wrist were made to match. With modern jewelry, the clasps were totally simple, usually just a common spring ring, screw barrel, or button-shaped clasp.

Even though modern jewelry's components were uncompromisingly severe, its golden gleam was warm. There was also an element of sensual, very unmachinelike play in the way the metal beads and chains could jostle against each other, or move slightly with the wearer's body.

The cult of the modern also had a surprising recruit—the unpredictable Schiaparelli, who put several classic modern jewelry designs on the map. In 1935 she made a heavy gold metal chain bracelet and necklace set with a padlock closure. The next year she did a beautiful bracelet set of gold metal balls, looking much like lumpy bunches of grapes. Her ball-and-chain bracelet, looking just like the real thing, was advertised as "polished pistons and fretted metal balls." *Harper's Bazaar* described it as having "mechanical splendor" and praised it as "the bolder, the better, the crueler, the more chic."

Not everyone was convinced that the modern machine mode was best, and a historical backlash flourished at the same time. New houses were copies of Early American and Georgian models, furnished with replicas of Chippendale and Hepplewhite treasures. Clothes, too, sought the past. Women donned the old-fashioned Victorian and Directoire styles, often accessorizing these outfits with modern jewelry.

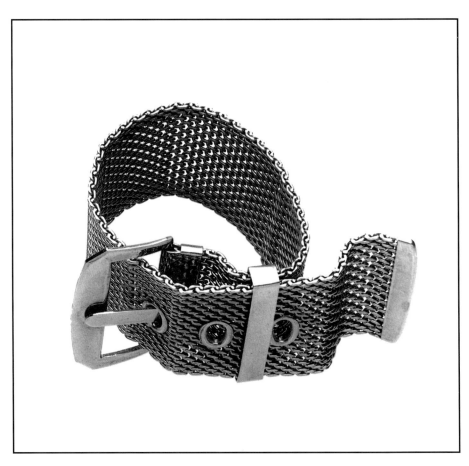

Metal clips and earrings (far left) display the streamlined style. Two-inch-wide metal bracelet (left) buckles like a belt; its design was attributed to Schiaparelli. An array of glamorous jewelry (top) fills a fashionable store window. Pair of matched plastic clips (top right) graced fashion's new focal point—the plunging back of a dress (bottom). Alternatively, clips were fastened on the dress straps.

CLIPS If the entire range of 1930s costume jewelry had to be represented by a single item, it would be the clip.

Clips decorated hat brims, cuffs, gloves, handbags, belts, the waist of a backless dress, shoulder straps, lapels, or the intricate flares and flounces of a décolletage. Chanel even showed clips attached to fur collars. With dress necklines a mess of complicated drapery, the clip was the perfect—the only—ornament that could be fastened to that flowing fabric without spoiling the line.

Clips were always worn in pairs of two, sometimes four at a time. They were usually identical twins: a variation was a large ornate clip accompanied by a smaller, simpler one. Clips came in all shapes, sizes, and a spectrum of materials, from cut stones to plastic to wood. Subject matter was infinitely varied, from animals to abstracts.

A New York store ad in *Dress Essentials* magazine in the spring of 1929 gushed, "Rhinestone clips for evening dress—Van Cleef & Arpels in Paris are responsible for the originals, which met with such success we felt called upon to get them copied instantly." Whoever did the clip first, it was probably first created in precious stones in Paris and then crossed the Atlantic to be copied in costume jewelry.

Slightly later, about 1935, came the combination, or "double" clip pins. The double clips contained two pins or clips, which could be worn two ways: locked together on their special metal bar, they were a single clip; unsnapped, the pins were worn separately. Hair ornaments, buckles, and even bracelets functioned in the same way. The Coro Company cleverly called their double clip combos "Duettes" and "Smart Sets." Although primarily a 1930s fashion fancy, clips, double clips, and combination clips continued to be worn as late as the 1940s.

NOVELTY NEWS

The 1930s were the heyday of wacky jewelry: odd subjects and strange materials—from the ridiculous to the sublime—were its characteristics. Women had plenty of pets locked up in their jewelry boxes. Dogs, cats, horses, deer, elephants, spiders—representatives of the animal and insect worlds were transformed into costume jewelry. They weren't the only unusual jewelry-box occupants, either. Sharing the space were cowboy and Indian brooches, fruit necklaces, and palm-tree earrings. With its crayon colors—even movable parts—novelty jewelry looked as if it could have been swiped off a birthday cake or stolen from a souvenir shop or a baby's crib.

Only a fevered humor could have persuaded the stylish woman to slap a 3-D horse pin on her jacket, a scallion brooch on her hat, button her dress with wooden tarantulas, and put plastic strawberries around her neck. And clearly, here was a woman who had a confidence born of whimsy. "By night we're brilliant—by day we're quaint," quipped *Pictorial Review* in 1930, describing their look. "Quaint" seems too mild a word for the styles these women adopted. The attitude was carefree and childish. One of the most talked about parties of the day was hostess Elsa Maxwell's "barnyard" party at the Waldorf-Astoria hotel. She had real hay and livestock dragged right into the ballroom as decor; the cows wore little felt booties.

The novelty style left its imprint on both fashion and accessories—everything from buttons, embroidery, and hats to couture clothing and jewelry. The style sprang from a mélange of influences, including Surrealist art, the easygoing, tropical style of California, and Walt Disney's wondrous cartoons. Its frivolous nature was also an uplifting antidote to the crisis of the Depression and the approaching shadow of war. Fashion was also an ingredient in novelty jewelry's appeal. For daytime wear, the black dress was the 1930s standard, and its simple silhouette and dark color were the perfect foil for novelty jewelry's often riotous colors and exaggerated shapes. Women's suits also came marching in. Military in cut, their wide lapels and wider padded shoulders provided a big space for big jewelry to conquer. And conquer it did: clips, pins, fobs, brooches, "gadgets," necklaces, and bracelets were created in a hard-to-miss super size. The varied materials the jewelry was made from were part of its charm; the roll call included plastics, crystal, copper, gold and silver metal, patent leather, wood, felt, nuts, cork, shells, beads, buttons, plastic, and porcelain.

Advertising called this jewelry "lapel loot," "gadgets," and "conversation pieces," although "conversation stoppers" was more like it. The jewelry was a scene stealer; a Macy's ad for a novelty pin counseled that a novelty hat pin would "rob comment from your rival's to your hat!"

Gadget jewelry and charm bracelets were aimed at the new college-girl market, as apparently their madcap whimsy helped coeds cope with the serious grind of study. More sophisticated women sought the fantastical, highly personal jewelry of Elsa Schiaparelli. And nobody had the corner on fashion hi-jinks like "Schiap." Schiaparelli made her mark with fashions and accessories that typi-

Pink flamingo brooch (above), inspired by the tropical attitude of Florida and California and the Duchess of Windsor's jeweled original; colossal plastic butterfly belt buckle (center).

PLASTICS The plastic jewelry of the period was hunky and chunky. The Marblette Plastic Company bragged that their jewelry "looks massive, feels light." It was massive because of the way it was manufactured: big, round-edged shapes were sturdy, and easier to remove from a mold than more delicate ones. A significant date in plastics history was 1934, when the injection molding machine enabled hundreds of jewelry pieces to be turned out at once. Plastic jewelry became plentiful—and cheap. New synthetics included transparent, colorless Prystal (1929), vinyl (1930), Lucite and Plexiglas (1936), and nylon (1938).

As plastic became more refined, it was available for the first time in vibrant colors—and color had fashion by the throat during the 1930s. This technological advance was due to the nature of phenolic resin itself, which didn't change the intensity of dye colors, unlike Bakelite colors. Candy-bright jewel tones were the most common 1930s plastic colors, which retain their vividness today. (Bakelite resin tends to yellow with age and exposure to sunlight; most of that synthetic's paler tones have now mellowed to a caramel ivory color.) Oddball, eye-jarring colors were de rigeuer for both jewelry and fashion (notably clothes made from rayon): reds were searing; green was an acidic chartreuse; and Schiaparelli created Shocking Pink. The color frenzy lasted until about 1943, when shortages caused by World War II limited the use of dyes.

Fabulous spill of fruits and vegetables (top): necklaces and brooches in giddy cartoon colors; robot-like boy and girl brooches (left) with a machine-inspired style. Slap-happy plastic novelties (right).

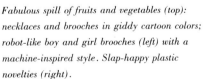

fied the hard chic of the 1930s: they were a mix of erotic daring, irreverent humor, and stylish high spirits. Photographer and fashion wise-eye Cecil Beaton said Schiap's designs had her "own particular form of ugliness." He added, "But then, fashions of today do not create beauties; in fact, beautiful women are at a disadvantage." Pretty wasn't interesting enough. The *Ladies' Home Journal* phrased it even more simply, asking their readers, "Do you want to look pretty, or smart?" Schiaparelli could have been pegged as the queen of trompe l'oeil, creating her versions of real objects—worn in the unlikeliest of places. Her fashion shows were anticipated like the punch line of a good joke. *Women's Wear Daily* reported the opening of a Schiaparelli collection in 1936: "Salvador Dali, the much discussed Surrealist painter, was present at the opening to see the youthful black suits with pockets like miniature bureau drawers with dangling handles covering the front of jackets, a hat with tiny coronet perched on top of a felt crown, gloves with red fingernails or blue veins painted on them." Schiaparelli put mauve lipstick on women's lips, fur gloves that looked like skunks on their hands, leopard fur on their shoes. Purses were replicas of telephones. Hats looked like shoes, airplane propellers, bottles of ink, or a lamb chop, complete with a white patent-leather frill over the end of the chop bone.

Schiaparelli originals: a transparent plastic collar necklace, crawling with metal bugs (right); flower brooch (opposite page).

SCHIAPARELLI Jean Cocteau described Elsa Schiaparelli in 1937, "Has she not the air of a young demon who tempts women, who leads the mad carnival in a burst of laughter?" Cocteau was among the circle of avant-garde artists, admirers, and collaborators that surrounded "Schiap," including Salvador Dali and Man Ray. Born to a wealthy Roman family, Schiaparelli made Paris her home. Her first fashions appeared in the late 1920s and the clients for her inventive looks included the Duchess of Windsor, Daisy Fellowes, Nancy Cunard, Mrs. Cole Porter, Myrna Loy, and Marlene Dietrich. Her costume jewelry, widely copied, was designed in collaboration with Jean Schlumberger and Jean Clément in the 1930s. In 1949 Schiap's fashions were produced for the first time for the mass market in the U.S.; she also licensed her name for American-made costume jewelry shortly afterward (which is signed "Schiaparelli" in script on the back). She died in 1973.

Schiaparelli, photographed by Cecil Beaton.

Her jewelry was just as varied, and, true to form, used experimental materials. "Materials should either be very beautiful, or odd and amusing," Schiaparelli said, in a *Fashion Accessories* interview. "I myself have used string, rubber, ostrich flues [feathers], in working out new ideas." An eyewitness account of her 1931 collection is a testimony to her innovative way with jewelry: "Belts were amusing; shirred leather; a coil of white enamel wire; wool elastic; red triangular mirrors. And colliers [necklaces] were equally original; thin white wood with china balls on the edge; red balls fastened to black cord; even an ostrich plume. The chef d'oeuvre was a large one of red radiators, very savage looking."

Much of Schiap's costume jewelry was designed to go with the theme of her fashion collections. For example, late in the 1930s her "Pagan" collection featured flower- and bug-bedecked jewelry and belts decorated with caterpillars. Her "Harlequin" collection of 1938 was accessorized with Pierrot brooches. That same year, Schiap did a brooch of a hand holding a flower (which had its roots in both Surrealist and East Indian sources), and it became one of the all-time popular jewelry items, endlessly copied. Her cherub pins were knocked off within scant weeks of their arrival in New York. The original cherub pin, imported from France, was $10. "First" copies cost $3.95. Finally, the cherubs were made available for 98 cents each.

For educated fashionables: a necklace of doll-sized school charms, all in plastic on a plastic chain (top); superstition necklace of plastic charms (bottom).

The taste for novelty that Schiaparelli started in Paris went westward ho. In the United States her quirky humor was married to a California sensibility, and their offspring was remarkable. This jewelry was a funky flotsam and jetsam of the odd nut, shell, bit of shellacked wood, and string. These pieces looked much like handcrafty, "I-was-there" vacation souvenirs or projects from summer camp. Creatures with acorn heads, painted-on eyes, and walnut-shell bodies were worn as brooches; circles of leather strung together made bracelets; a line of corks and plastic beads became a necklace.

California was fashion's fresh discovery, and it wasn't restricted to Hollywood glamor. "Of growing interest in the fashion world are Los Angeles-made accessories," bragged the *California Stylist* magazine. "All the romantic gaiety and characteristic color that bespeaks California seem concentrated in these smart accents. They have a definite personality that labels their identity as strongly as that of any other California product." Companies such as California Treasures and Hobby House capitalized on jewelry with a handmade look. Pins, clips, and buttons made of yucca wood, hand-painted with scenes of the California desert, were the specialty of another company. Other produce associated with the great state—

Painted nut necklace (top); plastic fruit harvest hangs from a necklace (bottom)

CHARMS

CHARMS The 1930s saw the re-birth of a classic: the charm bracelet. (Earlier on, Queen Victoria had her version, too.) Charm bracelets were targeted at a new customer, the college girl. Coeds became as famous on campus for their pounds and miles of charms and chains as for their saddle shoes and crewneck sweaters. On the college girl's wrist was a bracelet set with a tiny date book that opened; around her neck was a necklace of tiny rulers; clasped to her lapel was a tiny pencil and eraser clip.

Charms could be collected one at a time or purchased already assembled into "theme bracelets." Sample themes included "secretary's job," "sweethearts," "newlyweds," "Hawaii," "African jungle," "chess game," "orchestra," and "North Pole." A "New York City" bracelet jingled with a miniature cigarette lighter, champagne bottle, lipstick—and a telescope. Charms took note of current events and personalities. In 1935 Monocraft (later, the Monet Company) made charms of the Dionne Quints ("A sensation of History" said their ad) and Shirley Temple ("Bewitching Little Star").

During and after the Depression, there was a run on lucky charms, with subjects somewhat different than those of the luckies of the 1920s: 1930s charms had lucky lady bugs, elephants, scarecrows, horseshoes, monkeys, dice, and four-leaf clovers sealed in a clear plastic ball.

Some charms walked and talked—or nearly. A sample of articulated cuties included a mini-mailbox charm that opened and shut, an airplane with a propeller that whirled, a wagon with wheels that turned, whistles that "whistled," and a tiny tambourine that made a tiny noise. A heart charm as big as a fingertip opened with a tiny key. The 1939 New York World's Fair and the interest it stimulated in foreign countries inspired souvenir charms of Chinese, Dutch, and Mexican cowboy figures. America was represented by Paul Revere on his horse, covered wagons, showboats, and the New England whale. Glorious California inspired charm themes, too: stucco houses, palm trees, burros, and swordfish.

eucalyptus pods, pottery, and petrified wood—were all used as jewelry items. Even actress Bette Davis, honored as one of the country's best-dressed women, had a soft spot for native California baubles. The *Jeweler's Circular* described Bette's personal jewelry-box favorites: "With active sports togs, Bette likes nature pieces such as lei and bracelets of pi-aki, shells from Waikiki, a necklace of eucalyptus buds lacquered coral and lime, and iridescent pine cone chatelaines, lobster clips, hand-carved wooden puppy pins, a bracelet of rough gold nuggets."

Naturally, shell jewelry washed up on fashion's shore. Real sea shells, and carved mother-of-pearl pieces made tropical necklaces, bracelets, earrings, clips. These were au naturel or tinted, mixed with other tiny shells or sea motifs (sea horses, starfish, etc.) and strung on silk cords or chains. Twisted, multi-strand necklaces and bracelets of small shells were also favored, even by the non-beach set. Miami and Palm Beach had to take credit for these fads, and, tourist paradises that they were, shells didn't come cheap: a necklace cost $5; bracelets, $1.98. In 1939 nautical fashions were the theme, and "marine jewelry" was more promotable than ever.

What's certain from all this is that jewelry counters were hopping. "Bizarre and exciting novelty jewelry items create curiosity as well as buying interest, particularly among women who are ever looking for the new and effective. Grotesque designs seem to be favored. Masks, vegetables, animals of metals, woods, beadings, feathers and stones cause shoppers to stop and look and gain attention to the department," summed up *Dress Accessories* in 1938. Apparently, this outrageous, cute, silly jewelry inspired affection. Women frequently stopped by the jewelry counter to check out the newest, cleverest outrage. Under their breath, they might have been humming a few bars of "Ain't We Got Fun."

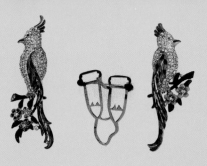

DUO CLIPS What fashion joined together, only fashion could draw asunder. Clips evolved from two separate pieces of jewelry into the "duo clip." When hinged together, the clips were worn as a single brooch. (Clips by Coro)

BLACKAMOOR PINS Diana Vreeland, Special Consultant to the Costume Institute of the Metropolitan Museum of Art and former *Vogue* editor, reminisces about her jewelry, "Have I ever shown you my little blackamoor heads from Cartier with their enameled turbans? Baba Lucinge and I used to wear them in rows and *rows* . . . they were the *chic* of Paris in the late thirties . . . the Cartier ones were quite expensive, but then Saks brought out a copy of them that sold for something like, in those days, thirty dollars apiece, and it was impossible to tell them apart. So I bought the copies and wore them with the real ones, like decorations—I was *covered* with blackamoors!"

NODDERS "Nodders," set on miniature springs, were a popular novelty gimmick in the 1930s. Tiny birds swung on a perch, flower petals trembled, bells tolled. With the wearer's footsteps, the jewelry jiggled. (Pins by Coro)

BUTTONS During the deep dark days of the Depression money was scarce for new jewelry or new dresses. Bright little buttons could make a drab dress cheerier. "Old costumes are reborn with new buttons." *The Delineator* trilled encouragingly "Buttons are frequently the most interesting point of a simple daytime dress . . . fasten yourself into your dress with lobster claws. Clasp your belt with scallop shells. Have sea urchins at your wrists and neckline. Oyster, clams, sand crabs, jingle shells and all the rest make buttons, buckles, clips studs." Buttons were made of practically anything: wood, hand-carved plastics, china, metal, crystal, mirrors, nuts, and old, mismatched earrings.

It was Schiaparelli who unbuttoned the traditional button, with her madcap array of decorative fasteners (including first-time couture zippers). "Cute as a button" was never more appropriate. Nearly anything that walked, crawled, swam, grew, or flew through the air was put to work as a button, from bananas to mirrors, butterflies to mermaids.

Like her jewelry, Schiap's buttons were created to go with her fashion collections: stars and moons for an astrological collection; clown-hat buttons (and a merry-go-round necklace) for a circus collection in 1938. Her button vocabulary also included safety pins, lollipops, coffee beans, and fish hooks. She did "toy" buttons too—little birds or hearts in 3-D wire cages, and little spinning tops that actually worked.

Besides the clever kind, buttons came in regular shapes and sizes, some hand-carved and hand-painted, like other plastic jewelry, with abstract or figurative designs. Buttons were also made into jewelry on their own: couturier Goupy made a necklace of intertwined enameled buttons in 1930. Leather-covered buttons (like those on sports jackets) also became a neck ornament. Crafts magazines featured "how-to's" for homemade button jewelry for the fashion-conscious artisan or scout troop.

RHINESTONES Rhinestones have a fabulously distinguished history; their creator was no less than the jeweler to the king of France. First known by the rather inelegant name of "paste" or "strass," rhinestones were created in the early 1700s by Georges Frederic Strass, an emigrant from Strasbourg working in Paris. He set lead-glass paste (colorless or tinted) into shoe buckles, brooches, aigrettes, and tiaras, which were popular with the aristocracy and anyone else who could afford their glitter. Paste wasn't as brilliant in those times as it came to be later on, when the silver foil backing that reflects shine was added.

The piled-high pompadour was in style in the late 1930s. Those richly coiled curls, stiff with pomade, made the perfect nest for a costume jewel or two. Hair combs, ornamented with glittery jeweled trim, also held up the swept-up hairdo in back. For a brief time, tiaras enjoyed a vogue. In 1939 Chanel showed tiaras of gold and silver flowers and leaves, matched with a necklace.

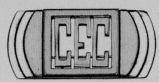

MARTHA SLEEPER America's home-grown answer to Schiaparelli's whimsies was Miss Martha Sleeper. By some accounts, Martha single-handedly brought California-style novelty jewelry, or "gadgets," into the limelight. Glamorous, Martha was perfectly cast for the part of a California jewelry designer—she was an actress. "A pretty and remarkable young lady, who would rather make bugs than star in moving pictures," was how *Collier's* magazine introduced her in 1938. A practical gal with no stars in her eyes, Martha had her reasons. She said, "Look, acting may be more remunerative, but the overhead of being an actress keeps me broke. Cars, mink coats, swimming pools—you know." So Martha took up jewelry making. Her medium was carved wood and plastic, and her territory was humor. She made jewelry ducks, cactus, grasshoppers, palm trees, pineapples, tropical fish, and lizards. A 3-D bird in a plastic cage was a pin. Plastic matchsticks made a necklace. A miniature picket fence with two black cats sitting on top became a bracelet.

Wild stuff, in bright-as-California colors, it got Martha noticed. At a Hollywood party, according to Martha, movie stars Dolores del Rio and Fay Wray "got very rude" about wanting to know where and how they could buy her unique animal jewelry. From then on, she was a star. Martha's jewelry was in such demand, she had to hook up with a company (D. Lisner of New York) and have it mass-produced. Fay Wray went on to star in a movie with a giant gorilla (King Kong), so perhaps Fay's interest in animal jewelry wasn't surprising.

MONOGRAMS Monogramed letters dangled from a fob, were made into a brooch, or clamped on a handbag as clips. They were made up in all kinds of materials, from wood to marcasite. Names and initials or letters spelling out memorabilia ("H-O-L-L-Y-W-O-O-D") were also strung on charm bracelet chains. Jean Patou made an elegant monogram necklace in 1932: a rounded metal plaque inscribed with letters, strung on fifty strands of tiny beads.

Modeled by
Martha Sleeper

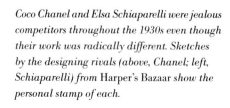

Coco Chanel and Elsa Schiaparelli were jealous competitors throughout the 1930s even though their work was radically different. Sketches by the designing rivals (above, Chanel; left, Schiaparelli) from Harper's Bazaar *show the personal stamp of each.*

L 40's

Launched with battleship charm bracelets, the 1940s ended with heavy rhinestone jewelry, fit for a costume party. Aside from its more earth-shattering consequences, World War II was responsible for splitting fashion into this before and after story. Unlike the 1920s and 1930s, this era saw fashion and jewelry take on a wholly American-made direction, a necessity caused by the wartime isolation of the U.S.

"War changes lots of things, doesn't it—even patches are patriotic now," mused a fashion editor in a 1942 radio interview, "today, patches and darns, mends and makeovers are more than just popular." The 1940s woman was grin-and-bear-it graceful. Holding up her part in the war effort gave her confidence, independence, a kind of patriotic strut. "The woman in overalls with a riveting gun in her hand will become as much a symbol of this war as the parachute trooper with his machine gun," bragged a *Mademoiselle* editorial.

The woman in overalls certainly appeared confident: the 1940s look of beauty was prepped with heavy strokes of eyebrow pencil, à la Joan Crawford. Lips were boldly brilliant with "Burma Red" or "Temple Fire" lipsticks. Fashion and the new female duked it out. "I often wear trousers in the street and the passersby don't seem to think it at all strange," claimed fashion designer Elizabeth Hawes.

The popular song "Bewitched, Bothered, and Bewildered" could have described fashion's outlook. There was a flurry of styles and accessories, each one odder than the next. In spite of shortages and "making do," there was glorious stuff to wear; most of it seemed to have a wisecracking, tough-gal appeal. A sampler included sandals, belts, bags, and jewelry in shiny gold—for daytime. There were turbans, leopard muffs, corsages, and clompy platform shoes. Fabrics came in Victory Garden colors; handknit sweaters and mittens were hot items.

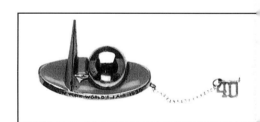

Sign of the times (opposite page): the "atomic starburst" brooch, in rhinestones and silver metal. Enameled sailor-boy brooch (left) was a patriotic accessory during the war, while the World's Fair pin (above) was a souvenir of happier times. Post-war, tailored jewelry was the style (above top right).

Earrings, bracelet, and shoe clips (above), hand-fashioned of sequins sewn on fabric, were an ingenious solution to the wartime jewelry materials shortage. By Arpad Necessories. Tiny hand-made hat (below), knit in red, white and blue, made a nifty lapel ornament, typical of the hand-crafted accessories that flourished during the war years.

Government regulations influenced fashion by restricting the amount of fabric that could be used for each garment, dress length (short), even the depth of a hem. Metal clasps and zippers had vanished (metal was needed for the war effort), leaving handbags looking like pillows and funny buttons holding things together. Leather was rationed—women teetered on four-inch-high cork wedgies. The attitude was "every little bit counts," and even elegants like *Harper's Bazaar* praised home-canned goods and home-sewn goodies.

With French industries ceasing production during the war (even French *Vogue* stopped publication from 1941 until 1945), Americans created clothes and jewelry for Americans. Even with Paris out of the picture, American designers still felt the sting of comparison: "Are we mice or designers?" quizzed one of them, loyally adding, " . . . resourcefulness and inventiveness are bred in the American soul. And so, too, is the creative spark, if we will but allow it to be kindled." California was the wartime fashion focus. A handful of Hollywood costume designers—Adrian, Travis Banton, and Edith Head—did their patriotic duty, creating for the average woman as well as starlets. Other designers worked under their own labels or for stores: among them were Elizabeth Hawes, Lily Dache, Nettie Rosenstein, Adele Simpson, Valentina, Claire McCardell, and Norman Norell.

Fashion went beyond style: it was also a patriotic choice. In 1941 *Mademoiselle* talked about her reader: "She'll have loyalties to neighboring nations that lead her to Chinese hairdos, Grecian drapery, screaming South American colors, and British Ambulance Corps prints."

Costume jewelry was just as pinched and peculiar in terms of style and material as fashion, but the "trinket" industry in the U.S. flourished. Business in 1945 was three times the figure of 1939. The reason? Working women had dough, and little to spend it on. Clothing was uninspiring or unavailable; accessories became all-important. "A lapel pin to be the bright spot on your stark I-85 suit, your trim beret, your basic black dress," dictated *Charm* magazine. Jewelry—in any shape or size—would sell. The only problem was there simply wasn't enough of it to go around (even stores were on a quota system).

In the 1940s costume jewelry was almost indistinguishable from the real thing, partly because of materials. Metal for jewelry making was restricted or prohibited during the war, so sterling silver and gold, both non-priority metals, were used to plate much of the costume jewelry. After the war, gold was dropped in favor of silver. Another factor that affected costume jewelry style was the lack of cut stones, beads, and pearls imported from Europe and Japan. A scarcity of those items led to tiny sized stones, or one-big-rock per jewelry item as a standard look.

PEARLS At the end of the 1940s artificial pearls made a comeback, a return orchestrated by Jacques Fath and Christian Dior, who showed luxurious multi-strand necklaces matched with dangling earrings and ropes of pearly bracelets. The vogue for pearls would last well into the late 1950s.

A renewed popularity for colored pearls could be attributed to fashion's new friend, the mink. "Make mine mink" was the sentiment in 1949, and accessories, including pearls, were color-matched to the silver-blue, champagne, golden, and blonde shades of this highly prized fur, as well as to the pastel tones that the mink was often dyed. Different colors of pearls could be mixed together in a single piece of jewelry—resulting in something like Indian corn.

Pearls were in such demand that in 1948 they represented 40 to 50 percent of all jewelry sold, reported *Kaleidoscope* magazine. Keyed to the dictates of dress, ever-adaptable pearls came as thick chokers or the longer, five-foot necklace, worn knotted close to the neck à la 1920s, or draped around the neck and anchored to the front of the dress with a big pin. By 1948 dresses were cut low in back, and pearls were worn backward—trailing tails of beads—by the sophisticated set. The conservative and the college girl preferred the regular single-strand pearl necklace, properly worn in front.

Bracelets matched the glory of the pearl necklace: triple rows of beads strung on flexible wire or knotted on string were common styles. Earrings were neat pearl buttons as well as more elaborate designs of dripping pearls mixed with rhinestones.

These pseudo-oyster gems didn't come cheap. A nine-strand pearl choker at the Hattie Carnegie boutique was a hefty $50—the price of a "good" ladies' suit at any other shop.

Jewelry manufacturers ad-libbed with substitutions, enriching the vocabulary of materials to include stones that were not in common use before the war: topaz, aquamarine, amethyst. Plain and baroque pearls and rhinestones, tinted in soft grays, were late 1940s additions.

Gold plating, plus real-looking semi-precious stones made costume jewelry more widely accepted. The *Jeweler's Circular* noted, "Costume jewelry, strange as it may seem, has helped popularize colored stone jewelry of the better grades. Many a woman who would have hesitated to wear bright colored jewels has been made aware of their beauty. . . . the 'new poor' are turning to this type of jewelry. . . ." Real jewels weren't to be flaunted. The semi-precious—or the look of it—was more in keeping with the mood of the war years.

To cope with the scarcities, costume jewelry had to make do. One of its most interesting "make do" items was novelty jewelry. *The New York Times Magazine* answered the question, "What is the last word in costume jewelry?" with a definition of the novelty genre: "Wood. Colored plastics. Shells strung on strings. Seeds and pods from Victory Gardens. And, perhaps most ingenious of all, jewelry made of driftwood, culled from the beaches on the West Coast to the Eastern Seaboard and studded with fake pearls and glass stones." This jewelry had a strange, home-made look, and—made in America from native materials—it had patriotic support. Never mind that it looked a little off. Novelties of the era also included cartoon characters inspired by Walt Disney and fantasy creatures: horse brooches made of wood, earrings and necklaces made from painted plaster, and ceramics.

War-related jewelry also had support. Sentimental reminders of the loved ones overseas were available as sweet good luck charms and lockets, or more sinister charm bracelets hung with fighting ships and tanks. At the end of the decade, the "snowflake" brooch or earring, a tailored jewelry standard, was now called "atomic."

Perhaps to escape the trauma of the war and soften the harshness of their military-cut suits, women turned to historical romance and especially to Victorian and Rococo fashions and costume jewelry. "Victoriana" was a straight copy of the original: chatelaines, lockets, and even hat pins were created in the same scale, trimmings (fake garnets, tiny pearls) and material ("antique" gold). The rippling Rococo/Directoire style bow and ribbon, usually in various-colored golds, was one of the most widely worn jewelry decorations. When it fell from favor toward the end of the decade, it was replaced by jewelry that was its temperamental opposite: the flamboyant glass bibs and wide collar necklaces of the Oriental style, launched in 1947 along with Christian Dior's New Look. The elegance of the Oriental style jewelry lasted right on into the next twenty years. When the good life was back, it was back with a vengeance: there were 3,294 country clubs in the United States in 1948, and a good thing, because now there was a place to wear that dazzle. Now that glamour was back to its rightful place on fashion's throne, crowned by rhinestones, all was right with the world.

TAILORED JEWELRY

In *The Lady in the Lake*, Raymond Chandler described the 1940s version of the hard-boiled female: "She wore a steel-gray business suit and under the jacket a dark blue shirt and a man's tie of lighter shade. The edges of the folded handkerchief in the breast pocket looked sharp enough to slice bread. She wore a linked bracelet and no other jewelry . . . she had a smooth ivory skin and rather severe eyebrows and large dark eyes that looked as if they might warm up at the right time and in the right place." That babe wouldn't have been caught dead wearing anything as romantic as a cameo or a locket. Tailored costume jewelry—the plain linked bracelet—was her badge of style. If she'd wanted to add a few more accessories in the same vein, she might have donned tiny gold hoop earrings and a simple snake chain around her neck.

Both the lady's jewelry, and her suit, were 1940s classics. They made a logical pair: the severe, man-tailored, padded-shouldered suit was the perfect foil for uncluttered jewelry.

Selection of simply shaped, gold-metal earrings (above). Pre-war tailored bracelets (right) were big and bulky gold-metal weights for the wrist. Single starburst earring (opposite page), made of pearls and gold metal.

Sleek and simple, tailored jewelry first developed as a type in the 1920s and 1930s, when it was tagged "modern." The 1940s retitled it "tailored," but in all its incarnations the jewelry shared a simple, direct shape and the idea that it was totally new—no ancestor worship or historical precedent was attached to its design. The word "modern" fell from fashionable lingo in the 1940s, perhaps because it smacked of the now passé streamline era. In spite of disowning its 1930s "modern" title, the jewelry still had a precise, machine-part look, and a smooth, textureless, shiny finish. Metal was the predominant material, especially gold-plated sterling silver or brass, which came in a range of colors—pink, green, or yellow.

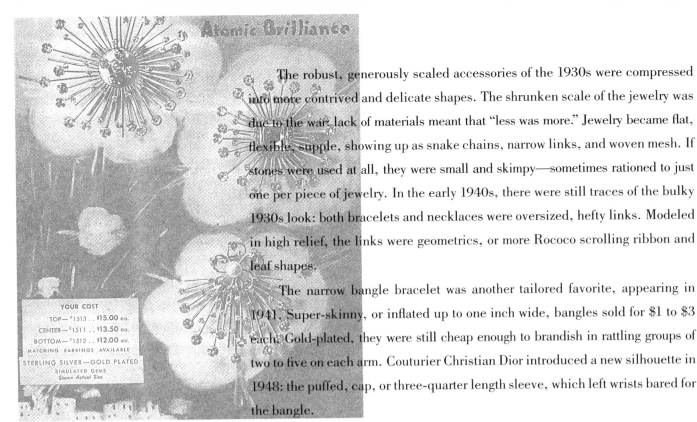

YOUR COST
TOP— #1513 . . $15.00 ea.
CENTER— #1511 . . $13.50 ea.
BOTTOM— #1512 . . $12.00 ea.
MATCHING EARRINGS AVAILABLE
STERLING SILVER—GOLD PLATED
SIMULATED GEMS
Shown Actual Size

The robust, generously scaled accessories of the 1930s were compressed into more contrived and delicate shapes. The shrunken scale of the jewelry was due to the war; lack of materials meant that "less was more." Jewelry became flat, flexible, supple, showing up as snake chains, narrow links, and woven mesh. If stones were used at all, they were small and skimpy—sometimes rationed to just one per piece of jewelry. In the early 1940s, there were still traces of the bulky 1930s look: both bracelets and necklaces were oversized, hefty links. Modeled in high relief, the links were geometrics, or more Rococo scrolling ribbon and leaf shapes.

The narrow bangle bracelet was another tailored favorite, appearing in 1941. Super-skinny, or inflated up to one inch wide, bangles sold for $1 to $3 each. Gold-plated, they were still cheap enough to brandish in rattling groups of two to five on each arm. Couturier Christian Dior introduced a new silhouette in 1948: the puffed, cap, or three-quarter length sleeve, which left wrists bared for the bangle.

Necklaces were as simple as a circlet of links or a flat chain ending in a tassel, made up in a neat, short, choker length. They were worn one at a time, unlike bracelets, which were worn extravagantly—en masse. The earrings that completed the tailored ensemble looked much like miniature, lobe-sized brooches, vaguely reminiscent in style of a cross between flowers, leaves, and a machine. And that ubiquitous classic—the hoop earring—came into its own.

The belt was a newly important accessory, mimicking the necklace and the bracelet, link for link. "Jewelry goes so far in adding a theatrical touch to blouses," observed *Fashion Accessories.* "It may be a metal belt with clanking coins or hunks n' hunks of bracelets . . . and always earrings."

Because of its gold plating, and its look-alike design (which mimicked the best of Cartier and Van Cleef & Arpels), for once costume jewelry could pass for the real thing—at least at first glance. Tailored jewelry had stones that were small and few, little detailed metal work, and the jewelry itself was a proper, could-be-real size. A popular weekly magazine summed up the situation in 1945: "To see what the trend is, you don't have to go to the fine jewelry shops. All you have to do is walk into that old copycat, the five-and-ten. There you'll see sophisticated sunbursts, and dome-shaped earrings and bracelets, replicas of the costly gold ones that are popularly studded with chips of turquoise, diamonds, and ruby. Elegant, not gaudy, is the word."

The 1940s tailored jewelry was a lightweight and somber contrast to the earlier 1930s modernistic pieces, which were characterized by the flashy excess of their size. Tailored jewelry had a fine, well-behaved character, and it was the approved accessory for working ladies in suits with its timid, unquestionable style and minimal variation. Restrained enough to pass for genuine precious jewelry, perhaps in the shaky days of the 1940s, this no-risk style provided some surety and comfort.

THE SUNBURST One of the most pervasive jewelry motifs—the sunburst—was created late in the era. It also went by the names "starburst," "comet," "snowflake," and "star." In 1945 it was advertised as "atomic." It did look like an explosion: radiating around a center circle (a pearl, a stone, or a glob of metal) was a spindly halo of rays. The rays could be tipped with a gem or a pearl; they could also be sharp, blunt, or flat spikes, or built up in multiple, 3-D layers.

The atomic sunburst was thorny and dangerous-looking, as appealing as a jeweled porcupine. An uneasy ornament, it twinkled on ears, wrists, and around necks. Atomic brooches were common decoration for lapel, dress front, and hat (pinned on a big brim just over the forehead). The atomic starburst cast its rays from the mid-1940s into the 1950s. (In its later incarnation, that atomic shape became a crossover, used as a design motif on fabrics, linoleum, dishware, and other products.)

NOVELTY AND PATRIOTIC JEWELRY

The 1940s gal didn't lose her sense of humor, even with her world turned upside down by the war. She needed humor, what with a waiting list for black lingerie and having to wear colored leg makeup in lieu of scarce silk stockings.

That "see-it-through" humor—and the make-do lessons of the war—ricocheted into fashion producing quirky, handmade-looking items.

Novelty jewelry plunged into the same spirit. There was a proliferation of oddball, seemingly ad-libbed baubles, of shaky quality and peculiar materials. Magazines even featured how-to instructions for creating jewelry at home, such as a knit ornament (a thumb-sized pair of mittens to wear on a lapel) or a necklace of gingham fabric glued over beads. Materials that were cheap and plentiful—cork, bits of real fur, feathers and leather; rice, beans, and pumpkin seeds; fish scales, straw, and ceramics—were used, often in combination.

By some stroke of marketing genius, these novelties were promoted as patriotic, American self-reliance items. At what other time in history would a necklace of red, white, and blue-painted walnuts rate as a fashion item? *Fashion Accessories* voiced the sentiment in 1941, "The costume jewelry industry has thrived and progressed entirely from home talent and originality . . . giving concrete evidence of the resourceful characteristic of American business."

California was the wartime capital of novelty costume jewelry. Stores fastened their interest on West Coast baubles once jewelry imports from Europe were cut off, and in 1941 sales of California jewelry to retail outlets shot up 35 to 50 percent. Department stores across the country launched "California" promotions to push native fashion and jewelry. The Carson Pirie Scott & Company store was typical: their 1944 "Native California Flair" promotion " . . . aroused much interest among Chicagoans in the colorful, light-hearted materials and designs presented."

The seeds and beads, and shells that made up this jewelry appeared to share a few characteristics with the "barbaric" jewelry of the 1920s. However, the allure of the 1940s pieces was markedly different: in the 1920s this rough jewelry was savage, primitive, and exotically daring: in the 1940s the same materials became amusing and "American."

Some of the 1940s jewelry flotsam and jetsam had romantic, tropical island origins. No less than the Duchess of Windsor herself sponsored the "island industries" of Eleuthera, in the Bahamas in 1942: the promotion of native-made seed jewelry was her attempt to help the island economy. Shells from places

Worn with great good humor, a painted wooden bulldog brooch (opposite page), complete with a metal-chain dog collar around its neck. Soft stuffed-leather hat-and-horseshoe pin (above); prickly coral-and-bead necklace and bracelet (below), designed for casual wear.

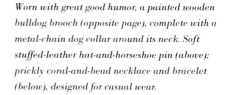

like far-off Hawaii were commonly used—glued into stiff, delicate little flower-like arrangements. (Shell earrings often had plastic clip backs—lightweight, inexpensive, and non-priority substitutes for metal clips.)

Other materials, such as pumpkin and squash seeds, weren't as glamorous. If jewelry designers had ransacked the mountains, the beaches, and the forests for materials, it looked as if they'd also checked the garbage. There were inspired souls who created necklaces from hand-carved olive pits and coffee beans (popular in 1941). Unlikelier still were strands of processed puffed rice, said to be "quite durable and dyed in many colors," according to a *Women's Wear Daily* report. Perhaps the maddest jewelry of all was made from macaroni. Not just a flash in the pan (or casserole), macaroni bracelets and necklaces, available in fashionable colors and in multiple or braided strands, were around for several seasons in the early 1940s.

Even lowly curtain trim was woven into jewelry. "Jewelry firms are taking up all sorts of yarn and cord, fringe and fishnet, to fashion spring novelties . . . and so you get collars of swagged loops of upholstery fringe, or a pocket piece which looks for all the world like a glorified curtain tassel . . . " noted a market report in 1941.

In addition to the rustic stuff, California gave the world cartoon character jewelry mainly inspired by Walt Disney's movies. Many of these novelties were made to move, another thank-you to cartoon animation. A doggie brooch had felt ears that flopped, a red fabric tongue that did likewise, eyes that moved, and a head that wiggled. The cast of Disney's 1940 film "Fantasia" (baby horses, Centaurs, dancing flowers) was transformed into wood and enamel pins and earrings, and by 1945 the Disney parade included Donald Duck, Mickey Mouse, Bambi, Thumper, and Jiminy Cricket and the gang, all copied in sterling silver charms. Snow White and her seven dwarves were also part of the charm bracelet lineup.

The sources for the novelty population were endless. The classic children's book, *Stuart Little*, published in 1945, sparked dainty little "Stuart" mouse pins, after its hero. (Tiffany & Company even did precious jewelry storybook character pins for grownups.) Sparkle Plenty (the baby from the *Dick Tracy* comic strip) became a pin. So did Harvey, the rabbit star of the 1945 Broadway play—later the movie—of the same name. The play *Oklahoma!* launched a "surrey with the fringe on top" brooch to wear, after the show's hit tune. In 1948 a pair of jeweled crowns made a best-selling comeback, this time commemorating the royal wedding of Princess Elizabeth of England. On a more somber note, birds and the dancing ballerina were also popular wartime images, representing flight and freedom.

Ceramics and wood were two of the most popular jewelry materials; leather, glass (Pyrex), and plaster were also used. Ceramics came with a crackle glaze or in plain bisque form (unglazed), and in multiple colors, even some incorporating 22K gold. Ceramic jewelry designers were as uninhibited as kindergard-

Tiny ceramic clock earrings (above); original character pins from Walt Disney's movie Fantasia *(below) made by the Authentics company.*

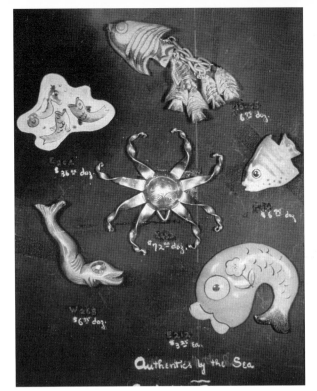

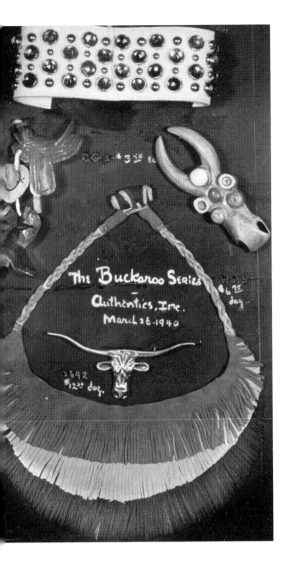

As originally presented by Authentics: ceramic
sea creature brooches (above right) and studded
leather bracelet, boots 'n saddle and cow-head
brooches, and fringed leather neckpiece (above
left); hand-carved and hand-painted wooden
cowboy brooch, standing four inches tall.

ners: a clown brooch wore a pasted-on lace ruff, Zulu warriors had yarn hair, Eskimos were bundled into fur parkas, and maidens were crowned with leather hats and braids.

Wooden jewelry had much the same silly subjects. Horses were a favorite, complete with round glass eyes, real leather bridle, and tossing yarn mane.

Leather was used ingeniously—often punched out into circles, studded with brass, and fastened to a leather rope to wear as a necklace and bracelet. Soft leather was also sewn and stuffed into toy character pins. *Women's Wear Daily* reported on another leather conversation piece in 1941, "A novelty is a big football pin with places for campus friends to write names or initials."

Because of wartime material restrictions, and the popularity of the "native and patriotic," plastic novelties weren't the stars they were in the 1930s. Clear Lucite became a 1940s standard as colors for plastic were limited. Lucite was commonly mixed with other materials, such as wood, leather, or ceramics, as well as with opaque plastics. "Aquapearl" (a pearly opaque plastic) was created by the Catalin company in 1940. The first Aquapearl collection was by American jewelry designer Martha Sleeper.

Still in service was "tell-a-story" or themed gadget jewelry. Usefulness was a key element in the 1940s. Practical necklaces and bracelets and pins dangled a tiny screwdriver, hammer, flashlight, saw, and nails or a plastic compass, pen point, pencil, and ruler; sewing thread and thimble; or fake lipstick, mirror, and mascara brushes. There was even a tiny blackboard brooch made of patent leather, complete with an even tinier chalk and eraser.

For leap year of 1944 costume jewelry rallied with a series of question-mark jewelry (as in "pop the question"). There were "?" earrings and pins, all sporting a tiny heart in place of the dot on the question mark.

After the war was over, the cartoon sweetness of novelty jewelry completely vanished, along with the oddball materials it was made from; these souvenirs were now regarded as hopelessly old fashioned.

World War II set a precedent: it was not only fashionable to wear costume jewelry, it was downright patriotic. Jewelry inspired by the swell of patriotism wasn't pretty stuff to look at, but it didn't have to be: it was a statement of support and hope; a memento; remember-the-men-overseas, red, white, and true blue. Wives, sisters, mothers, sweethearts, and friends proudly wore dog-tag bracelets, star-spangled flag pins, Uncle Sam earrings, and necklaces emblazoned V-for-Victory. Patriotic jewelry was sold all across the country, in the high-priced as well as the five-and-dime stores. Everybody did their part: even the elegant Bonwit Teller store featured patriotic jewelry in their Salon de Couture in 1940.

Costume jewelry was the patriotic choice during World War II—no matter what the wearer's fashion persuasion. Selection of metal brooches and ID bracelets by Trifari. Opposite page: plastic jeep brooch (top) and red, white, and blue stone flag and League of Nations enamel flag brooches (bottom) by Coro.

WARTIME TROUBLES In the eyes of the U.S. government, baubles and bangles were hardly a wartime priority. There was a limited amount of metal available, and most of it had to go to the fueling of war machinery. In 1942, the government restricted and/ or prohibited tin, copper, nickel, and zinc—the ingredients of "white metal," costume jewelry's primary material. The government also requested that surplus metal be turned in; some jewelry companies complied, turning over metal scrap as well as old jewelry pattern molds (later regretted, since they were nearly impossible to replace). Jewelry companies were also restricted to a materials quota, scaled to the volume of their business before the war. In turn, they put the stores on a quota for jewelry.

Weary of wartime austerity, women were willing to buy almost any luxury item, and a hefty price tag was no obstacle. In 1943, the price for a big, gold-plated sterling silver piece of jewelry, loaded with a single large stone: $22.50 for a bow-knot pin; $20 for a ring; $47.50 for a bracelet. Companies reported that even at $100, jewelry would find a buyer.

Manufacturers turned to substituting other materials: white metal was replaced by sterling silver, beginning in 1942. Costume jewelry was both made and plated with silver as well as gold. Like "precious" jewelry, it was available in yellow, pink, white, or green gold; a mix of two or three of these tones on a single piece was a standard 1940s look.

The materials crunch also affected availability of cut glass stones. Before the war, nearly all rhinestones, cut glass, and the like were Czechoslovakian or Austrian imports; artificial pearls were from Japan. The war totally cut off these sources. The jewelry companies that had a backstock of supplies used them sparingly. Others hoarded their stones and pearls, now precious as diamonds, as prices skyrocketed. For example: cut round stones had a pre-war price of 4 cents a gross; by 1946 the price was 60 cents. Larger sized, fancy cut stones were as high as $10 a gross, when available. With stones so dearly priced, a rhinestone "black market" developed in the United States. Quantities of rhinestones would change hands again and again, sold by speculators. Acetate stones, sometimes set in a metal "cup" to increase their shine, were a dull and short-lived replacement for the glitter of real rhinestones.

Patriotic jewelry sparked spirits at home, too. "Courage" became a perfume in 1942. Revlon's lipsticks were "Rosy Future" and "Bright Forecast." Fashion magazines beat drums in sympathy, featuring page after page of neat, military-style suits and trousers for women. The *California Stylist* contrasted the old attitude (the 1938 debutante's) with the new situation: "No more does the picture of Brenda Frazier in a street dress mean anything to America's new woman who is a welder, an airplane spotter, a Red Cross volunteer . . . "

There were two types of patriotic jewelry: exact replicas of military motifs and "novelty," take-off items. The military insignia were duplicates of the real ones worn by fighting men. Women wore them as lapel pins, tie tacks, and earrings as early as 1940. They were of plain and enameled metal, sometimes sparkling with red, white, and blue stones. (Interestingly, even then they were called "collector's items.") ID bracelets also carried military insignia. To show the military rank of their loved ones, women wore chevron pins, from the private's stripe to the general's star. This jewelry was so popular that nearly every costume jewelry company had a line of patriotic commemoratives. One American company alone offered over 200 different items. Flags, the eagle, Uncle Sam, bugles, the Liberty Bell, and the Statue of Liberty were all popular. America's First Lady, Mrs. Roosevelt, wore a League of Nations pin that the Coro Company created for her.

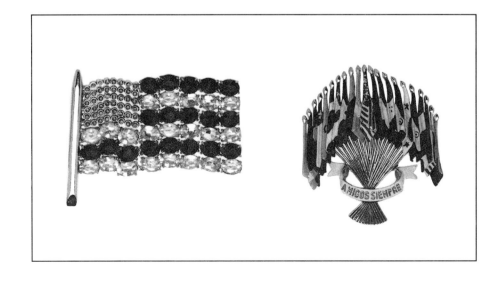

*The religious cross (opposite page) was made up
in a variety of materials, from metal to plastic.
War novelties with a humorous twist: a selection
of whimsical plastic pins (above). Metal link
bracelet (center) confidently brandishes a hefty
one-inch square "V-for-Victory" charm.*

Some of these ornaments were marketed as "jewelry aid," with all funds
raised from sales donated to individual war relief efforts. A line of "Allies" support jewelry offered the crossed American flag and the Union Jack, going for
$2.50, as well as "V" lapel pins for 50 cents (proceeds went to Great Britain); the
thistle, $1.50 (Scottish Clans Evacuation Plan); the rooster pin, $2.00 (Feder-
ation of French War Veterans); the windmill pin, $2.00 (Queen Wilhelmina of
Holland Fund); and mushroom pin, $1.00 (United China Relief).

There was also an intriguing species of patriotic jewelry with a "code,"
continuing the tradition of gadget jewelry of the 1930s. For example: a necklace
was strung with a miniature carrot, apple, ear of corn, pepper, pea pod, tomato,
and a beet. The message behind this garden variety? A reminder: eat your daily
vitamins. Air raid warden jewelry was just as clever. Bracelets and brooches were
hung with a miniature helmet, flashlight, whistle, screwdriver, and flag insignia—all the equipment a girl needed for an emergency. Replicas of President
Roosevelt's cigarette holder and Winston Churchill's cigar were crossed into a
victory "V" lapel pin. "MacArthur Heart" jewelry debuted in 1942. A giant, four-
inch red plastic heart swung from a red plastic key, symbolizing "The Mac-
Arthur heart has the key to our liberty and his heart and soul are with us." "Pearl
Harbor Beauties" was the unlikely name for doll-like wooden pins, dressed in
yarn hula skirts. Miniature wooden WAC and WAVE figures, outfitted in felt
uniforms and tiny leather handbags, were ready to be pinned on a suit lapel.
Charm bracelets could hold an arsenal of war-related items: soldiers, sailors,
machine gun, jeep, B-12 bomber, anti-aircraft gun, Sherman tank, flying boat,
airplane, hand grenade—even the atom bomb. It was hard to imagine feeling
chic, instead of heavily armed, wearing those battle symbols around a wrist.

In the late summer of 1940 the "V for Victory" motifs swept the country.
Anything that could accommodate the letter V was branded with it: belts, gloves,
handbag, compact, jewelry, cigarette case, hanky, sweater—even bobby socks
were V-monogrammed while customers waited.

Sentimental jewelry was also wildly popular, most of it appearing as variations on the hearts and flowers of the Victorian originals. Lockets and pendants
concealed tiny photos behind their hinged front. Religious crosses were faithfully worn. For good luck, there was the four-leaf clover, the wishbone, and two
hands clasped in friendship. Once peace was declared, it was all over. Sentimental and patriotic jewelry couldn't be given away. Woe to the store with a surplus of hand-grenade charms!

"THE NEW LOOK" ORIENTAL

Like Sleeping Beauty, fashion awoke from its slumber after the war. Couturier Christian Dior played the role of rescuing prince. In 1947 his collection, dubbed the "New Look," was an eye-opener. After the makeshift fashions and skimpy jewelry of wartime, Dior offered an elaborate stylishness. The old padded shoulders lost their stuffing and became soft and sloping. Waists were tight and tiny. Skirts ballooned over petticoats. Wickedly low-cut necklines curved and plunged. The New Look was the postwar look for ladies around the world, and "Dior" became a household word.

Jewelry needed the same touch of magic to revive it. Dior delivered: he brought back big, bold rhinestones, made up into Oriental bib necklaces and massive chokers. Dior wasn't the only one with his mind on the lavish. Another couturier in Paris, Jacques Fath, created elaborate bib necklaces and multiple-strand bracelets made out of pearls.

Thanks to a combination of factors, the bib necklace—the "Oriental" or "Indian"-style stunner of the 1930s—became a 1940s favorite. While the 1930s necklace was composed of gold metal and semi-precious looking beads, the 1940s version did a twist on that formula, adding rhinestones, "jet," pearls, and clear glass beads. Dark, strong-colored stones, notably a smoky gray, a pale caramel, and a cat's-eye-yellow topaz were introduced. Baroque pearls also took on the coloring of these new stones, and came in pale-to-deep gray, sophisticated shades reminiscent of the "gunmetal" pearls of the late 1920s. The trio of faux rubies, emeralds, and sapphires were also an elegant combination in the Oriental neck-laces. These treasures were shaped into deep rounded bibs and V-shaped collars. Flat, flexible necklaces, they were often edged with a shivering stone or pearl drop fringe in front. In addition to the bibs, simply designed, wide dog collars of cut stones were a late 1940s jewelry innovation, apparently introduced simulta-neously by Dior and Fath. These overscaled and never-believable stone collars nestled around the neck like icy lightning.

The size of the jewelry elements was news: the stones were showstoppers, only slightly smaller than dimes. This theatrical jewelry—fashion's fantasy of an Indian princess—was in no way real, or even trying to be. Comparing the 1940s Oriental-style jewelry to the 1930s work points up another difference between them: both shared the bib format, but the 1930s necklace was displayed against cloth, usually a high-necked black dress. The Oriental style of the 1940s had a different drama: the new plunging necklines were the perfect frame for the opu-lent glitter of this jewelry, worn against bare skin. Another variation was the shawl-collar necklace: studded with multi-colored stones, it was designed so it could be turned around and worn front to back.

Giant rhinestone collar (above) dates from the early 1940s; this opulent style would not be seen again until the end of the decade, photographed by Louise Dahl-Wolfe (opposite page, above) and featured in sketches (below).

The influence of India on fashion in the United States during the 1930s continued to affect 1940s jewelry, interrupted during the war, and then revived with renewed vigor—its exoticism untouched. India was also put in the spotlight in 1947, when it gained independence from Great Britain. Clothing styles during the 1940s didn't fall under India's influence, although the Duchess of Windsor had an antique sari cut up and re-made into an evening dress and turbans enjoyed a mild vogue.

Oriental jewelry—the stylistic descendant of the 1930s Oriental accessories—was stopped by the war. In 1940, the exclusive Hattie Carnegie boutique in New York, which set fashion for the rest of the country, unveiled a line of East Indian themed jewelry and clothing. "Rare, beautiful Indian jewelry of ancient potentates inspired a captivating group of modern costume jewelry at Hattie Carnegie which was featured as an important part of the fall showings," described *Fashion Digest* magazine. "Many costumes were created in the Oriental mood as dramatic foils for the jewelry." Carnegie's chief designer at this time was Norman Norell, later well known on his own. Unfortunately, none of the jewelry he created had his name attached: pieces were only stamped "Hattie Carnegie" on the back.

At the same time as Carnegie's Indian showing, there were other sightings of similarly themed jewelry. A Macy's store ad in August 1940 displayed a bib-style necklace, a hat-tassel clip, and a pin—all of rhinestones, described as "stupendous." The ad's copy was tinged with imagery of the war in Europe: "women will adore these fabulous fake pieces! Like rockets, they'll shine on jet black hats. Like TNT they'll emblazon your lapel . . . ignite your costume!" The ad's last word—drawing on the Indian inspiration—was "guaranteed to make you look like the Maharanee herself . . . for very little!" And very little it was, too: the triple-decker necklace of stones was $16.44. At that time, rhinestones were still plentiful, and reasonably priced. Postwar, a similar necklace would cost as much as $72.

Although rich jewelry was primarily an end-of-the-decade fashion, the attitude that led to its comeback had been nursed all along during the war. *California Stylist* reported in 1943, "The industrial workers are contrasting their denims to the sexiest black lace dresses on the market, cashing their war checks in the best stores and buying the snazziest cocktail togs." Oriental-style jewelry wasn't for the ingenue; it was jewelry for a woman.

The voluptuous jewelry that might have matched this fashion escapism wasn't manufactured during the war, for obvious reasons: those precious stones and pearls, mostly European imports, weren't available. However, even if the stones had been available, it's doubtful whether their flashiness would have suited the mood of the period. "Any frou-frou, any extravagance in line and material seemed, and was, incompatible, like evening clothes in day-light," quoth *Vogue*, in 1946. Exaggerated jewelry had to be postponed until Dior came along with a look that would influence jewelry styles for the next twenty-odd years.

ROMANTIC JEWELRY

"In this 24 hours-a-day life, there is an opportunity for every woman . . . to dress for war or escape," pronounced the *California Stylist*, mid-way through the 1940s. Practical, sensible—even slightly dowdy—clothing was de rigueur for women during the day, when some of them filled in for absent manpower, working at rough jobs. Evening wear was a different story, and women did their best to transform themselves into a feminine vision. Dressing for romance meant bows, frills, fluff. A woman could take her pick between two historical fashions—the Victorian style and the Rococo flourishes of the nineteenth-century empress of France, Eugénie. These styles existed side-by-side, and were an influence on both fashion and jewelry. *Smart* magazine pointed out in 1941, "Last year's hat may be too old to wear to the movies, but if we go back half a century—or even two or three centuries—we may pick up something which can be worked into the newest idea of the season." The 1940s were loose with historical accuracy, and both the Victorian and the Rococo styles were generally lumped together as "romantic." These styles dominated fashion in the 1940s until 1947, when the clean radicalism of Christian Dior's New Look extinguished their fussy femininity.

Victorian Modern

Fashion got the message: "*Gone With the Wind* is causing a magnificent splash in the cinema sea, and as an influence on women's dress it has created a great stir in the pool of fashion," gushed the *New York Times Magazine* in 1940. Magnificent splash or not, the *New York Times* wasn't exactly prophetic, since Victorian revival styles (especially in costume jewelry) had been around for some time prior to *Gone With the Wind*. Both the 1920s and the 1930s fashions had used Victorian motifs. Now, in the 1940s, their version was updated, and the fashion and jewelry used the term "Victorian Modern."

It wasn't just the movies that fueled historical escapism: *Fascination* magazine noted that one of the favorite ladies' novels, circa 1946, was the bodice-ripper *Duchess Hotspur*, the story of a passionate period heroine.

In real life, women grabbed the chance to dress like leading ladies. Evening clothes were luxurious: brocades, damask, heavy satins, taffeta—all non-restricted materials. "Victorian" fashions also encompassed the same elements found in the Rococo/Directoire style of the time, notably panniers, padding, peplums, lace and ruffles, hats with veils. Victorian modern jewelry wasn't only worn with period evening clothes. It was a complement to the rather severe, masculine-looking suits of the day.

Watching the silver screen, women could dream: there was Ingrid Bergman, lavishly costumed in the Victorian-era film *Saratoga Trunk*. Bette Davis played a Victorian governess in the movie *All This and Heaven, Too*. Her period costumes offered "interesting style points: bonnets, parasols, the tiny waist, full skirt," according to *Smart* magazine. There was one big difference in the way the 1940s woman wore Victorian jewels: while the modest Victorian maiden put jewelry over a buttoned-up, high-necked dress, the 1940s babe delighted in low-cut, revealing necklines.

In the 1930s, Victorian jewelry had that era's sensibility imposed on it, resulting in a clunky, heavy-looking style that was slightly campy. The 1940s preferred a more faithful duplication of the Victorian original—sometimes a direct copy. In fact, the more accurate, antique-y and heirloom-ish the jewelry looked, the better. Following those Victorian originals, costume jewelry used imitation amethysts, rubies, garnets, jet, and tiny pearls. Sparkling cut stones were only sparingly used. Gold mesh and delicate filigree were made up in dull "antique" gold, the favored material; pink and bright yellow gold and silver were also used.

The motifs of 1940s jewelry were a steal from the old Vic: cherubs, scrolls, garlands, leaves, tiny flowers, the cameo, and the cross. The sentimental was smiled upon, and fobs, stickpins, bar pins, and lockets were all resurrected.

The appetite for the nineteenth-century motifs also brought back the chatelaine. As made by the Victorians, the chatelaine was a brooch or bar pin that dangled useful objects (tiny scissors, pencils, etc.) from short chains. In the 1930s, the same idea became novelty "gadget" brooches. In the 1940s, the chatelaine format was the same: dangling from a brooch, bar pin or clasp were the necessities of modern life—keys, coins, bus tokens, pencils, miniature picture frames, and address book. Also practical was the "freshen up" chatelaine, outfitted with a Lilliputian mirror, compact, lipstick, and pillbox. (Bracelets also held similar goodies, or a selection of Victorian charm knock-offs.)

The chatelaine was also slightly transformed in the '40s: two small pins were connected by a flexible chain, worn draped across the bosom. The chains were also made exaggeratedly long (up to 16 inches), worn over the top of the shoulder, pinned front and back. Another variation was to fasten one pin at the waist and the other up over the shoulder. These chatelaine chains could also be heaped with charms like a charm bracelet.

Victorian earrings were part of the picture, thanks to the fashion for ear-baring upswept hair. Like other Victorian-era jewelry, earrings in the 1940s were often exact replicas of the originals: small, delicate drop earrings, usually dangling a tiny drop stone, pearl, or bit of filigree.

Victoriana bred another revival: the small precariously worn hat. Unless anchored down with a hat pin—that bit of old-fashioned weaponry—those tiny toppers would slide right off the upswept hairdo. Women would buy a matching pair of hat pins: one to secure the hat, the second to stab through a lapel. Those pompadour hairstyles also needed their very own jewelry—combs, jeweled Victorian combs—to keep that upsweep upswept.

Victorian revivals: bracelet with a plaque of cherubs (above) of faux semi-precious stones and pearls; locket and a keychain (to wear on a lapel; below). Two hands of friendship (right) hold tiny book for photo inserts.

Rococo

As had been the case in the 1930s, the revival of Rococo fashions (or "Directoire" as it was also called) in the 1940s did only lip service to Eugénie's signature look; her jewelry was a more accurate copy. Dresses exhibited a high waist, cap sleeves, narrow skirt, very low cut neckline. This silhouette was broken up with the bravado of a peplum, a small bustle, a pannier, and draped detailing. Even hair was upswept into a stiff-curled pompadour.

Like a movie monster that kept coming back to haunt a heroine, Eugénie's Rococo jewelry was revived again. Its frivolous, curved shapes and ribbons worked as a contrast to the stiffness of the 1940s fashions. Unlike the Rococo jewelry of the 1930s, this time around it lacked a certain luxe. Design elements were the same in both decades: looped scrolls, swags, sprays, ribbons, curved lines, bowknots. Figurative elements were also added in the '40s: the dancing ballerina, fantasy flower shapes and bouquets, feathers and sunbursts, all done in twisted ribbons of metal. Generally, the 1940s Rococo was more three-dimensional, more exaggerated, less generous than the 1930s pieces. "Metal is curved, flared, domed, or 'tied' to capture a feeling of motion and activity," was the description a jeweler gave the style. The bottom line was that both clothing and jewelry had a skimpy angularity that the swirls of metal and fabric couldn't disguise.

The bowknot and the flower spray were two of the decade's most common jewelry motifs. The bowknot can be traced directly back to its eighteenth-century original, called a "sévigné" after the Marquise de Sévigné. In the 1930s, it was a lazy ribbon bowknot; in the 1940s, it became a tightly tied whiplash. The flower spray was also reincarnated, usually as a brooch. The design was highly stylized, commonly a bunch of flowers, or even a single bloom, stem tied with a loopy ribbon bow. Sometimes the flowers became ribbons or bowknots. Sometimes the ribbons looked like feathers or flowers. The ribbons, feathers, and flowers were all frozen in an orgy of twists and curls.

During the war years, costume jewelry and precious jewelry were near look-alikes. Even the cheaper costume model's ribbons of metal were frequently plated in genuine gold (pink, green, yellow), or silver and took a super-high polish. A mix of several colors of gold on a single piece was common. Both jewelry types shared a limited wardrobe of look-alike stones, too: topaz, aquamarine, amethyst, and ruby were the favorites, real and faux. Rhinestones weren't used quite as often: hard to come by and expensive, their flashiness didn't quite suit the style. These cut stones were sparingly used: a single small-to-medium sized, square-cut stone per piece was typical, centered in a nest of flailing flowers or ribbons.

After the war, Rococo jewelry vanished; it had become a sad reminder of wartime. The style was also eclipsed by the glittering, gem-laden jewelry coming out of Paris, the creations of Dior and Jacques Fath. Next to these dazzlers, the Rococo style looked rather skimpy, and clumsily old-fashioned.

Curving Rococo pins (opposite page), in pink and gold metal, featuring typical square-cut stones. Variation of the same brooch (above) by Napier.

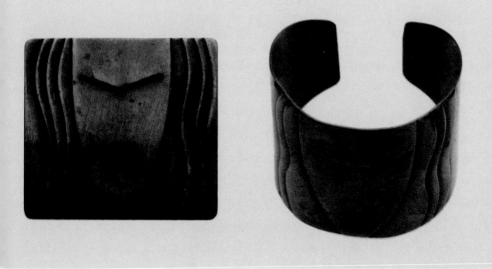

MEXICAN/INDIAN JEWELRY

The gush of good feeling for the United States' "good neighbor" policy made Latin American countries popular amigos in the early 1940s. Promotion for the land south of the border was heavy: Hollywood created film stars such as Carmen Miranda and Maria Montez (who faded out after World War II). The samba and the rhumba were the dances and the music of the moment. Fashion followed, offering off-the-shoulder, ruffled peasant blouses, and full skirts in bright "fiesta siesta" colors, along with hoop earrings, wide belts, and huarache sandals. "Warm Tamale" make-up was Coty's contribution to beauty.

The taste for this new exotica extended to jewelry from South America and Mexico, as well as to American Indian art. During the 1940s native, handmade silver jewelry was a patriotic purchase. (The vogue for "handmade" artisan jewelry had begun in the 1930s with the popularity of Scandinavian architecture, furnishings, and the silver work of Georg Jensen.) Silver also became standard for costume jewelry, too, due to the shortage of brass and white metals. The combination of these two factors changed the look of jewelry in general. According to the prophecy of Vera West, costume designer for Universal Studios, "Smaller and more finely wrought sterling silver necklaces, lapel pieces, and brooches will take the place of the fabulous bibs, chains, and hunks of brass of the past seasons."

Super-sized sterling silver flower brooch (opposite page), with a center of topaz glass. Copper cuff and charm bracelets, brooches, and a necklace (above and right). The "faces" have moveable parts. All by Rebajes.

The individual credited with popularizing Mexican silver was an American architect, William Spratling. While he was in Mexico researching a book, Spratling stumbled upon the village of Taxco, formerly a silversmithing center. Only three elderly men in the entire town still had the skills to work with silver, but it was enough for Spratling to revive the business, and by 1941, Taxco had 70 silversmithing shops; there were 122 craftsmen in Spratling's workshop alone. Spratling himself designed the jewelry that carried his name, using historic Mayan/Indian motifs.

SANDCASTING Take a look at the back of a piece of jewelry; if the metal is lumpy, thick, and looks slightly clumsy, chances are it was made by the sandcasting method. A surprisingly primitive technique, sandcasting was the manufacturing method used for most metal costume jewelry until the late 1940s, when the rubber mold method replaced it. Both sandcasting and bronze mold casting were used for jewelry made of silver-colored "white metal," the most common and inexpensive material. (The lost wax method is used only for casting brass and real silver and gold.)

In sandcasting, one side of a handcarved jewelry model was pressed into a box of slightly dampened, hard-packed sand. After the sand was dry, the model was lifted out, and the opposite side of the jewelry was pressed into a second box of sand. Then, a groove was made in each sand box, running from the top of the box to the empty jewelry mold crater. The two boxes were clamped together; molten metal was poured through a hole in the box, running down the groove in the sand to fill the two-sided jewelry impression. After the metal cooled and hardened, the two boxes were separated, and the finished jewelry was lifted out.

The piece of jewelry was then cleaned, filed, and sometimes jigsawed to smooth the rough edges. Stones and trim were then added individually. More expensive jewelry had (and still has) stones set in tiny prongs by hand; cheaper jewelry has stones glued in place.

"Spratling of Mexico" jewelry became so popular that stores across the country set up special Spratling boutiques or Mexican silver jewelry counters. Ever since Spratling's day, signed pieces of Mexican jewelry have been more valuable than unsigned ones. Some Mexican jewelry is stamped with the name of the designer (not the maker) on the back, but many pieces have no signature at all. This identification can vary from full name to first name to initials only. Early Spratling pieces were stamped "WS," with a bell shape, and "Hecho en Mexico," while later work was generally unmarked.

Other silversmith artists' signatures to look for include Antonio Pineda (sometimes signed with a crown), Frederick Davis (FD), Los Castillo, Héctor Aguilar (HA), and Margot de Taxco, an American who worked in Taxco from 1940 through the 1950s.

American Indian silver jewelry was also sought after, perhaps part of the patriotic spirit of the war years. "The arts and crafts of the Indian are a natural part of our American culture, and it is natural that they should be turned to for design inspiration at a time when patriotic fever runs high," preached *Women's Wear Daily* in 1946. In 1941 the Museum of Modern Art in New York held an exhibition of Indian art, featuring murals, pottery, weavings, and jewelry. This exhibition was influential: "All our important American stylists are hounding the museums in the East, going back to old parchment and early Indian lore to find inspiration for current fashion. They are not fads or fancies, but a solid background on which to sell American fashion and designs," reported *Fashion Accessories* in 1941. *Vogue* headlined Indian jewelry in a special "Americana" issue. Department stores offered moccasins, shawls, and Indian "broomstick" skirts (which were sold wrapped around a broomstick, the Indian way, to preserve their pleating).

Jewelry companies reported that sales of authentic Indian silver jewelry doubled from 1940 to 1941. Prices went up, too: in 1930, silver was 28 cents an ounce; a concha belt was $20. By 1941, a notable piece of Indian jewelry was up to $100. Native, and not-so-native materials were incorporated into authentic Mexican and Indian jewelry. Turquoise, "California jade," obsidian, tortoise, Mexican opal, tiger eye, moonstones, and amethysts were all used; coral was a postwar introduction.

The boom in genuine Indian jewelry, made by hand, also caused a boom in imitations. Manufacturers turned out "Indian" jewelry with strange inauthentic plastic and glass stones and design motifs taken from the original work. To stop the copies, the United States Indian Bureau put a ban on imitation, mass-produced Indian jewelry; copies could not be labeled as "genuine Indian handmade." Manufacturers got around the ban by calling their imitations "Indian made."

Department stores went so far as to send their own jewelry representatives to Mexico to work with the Indian craftsmen on designs. According to *Women's Wear Daily*, the reason was simple, "They wanted jewelry made in Mexico, but tailored to the American taste." That American taste made for some unusual hybrids, such as "Chinese" and "Danish"-looking Mexican silver jewelry.

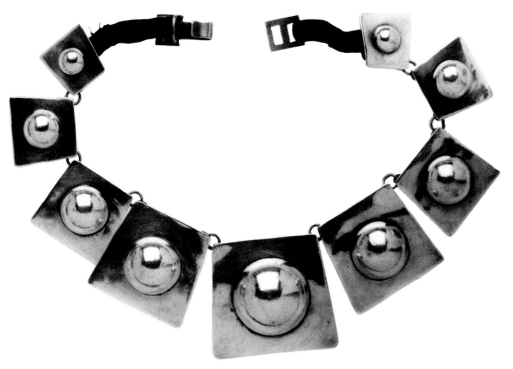

Opposite page: Pair of silver bird earrings (above) have amethyst eyes; fantastic bird brooch (center) of silver and onyx, signed "WS." Bold necklace of silver squares threaded on a suede ribbon (center), signed "WS." Below: made-in-Mexico cuff links with "Egyptian" motif (left); cross pendant (center), inlaid with chips of turquoise and onyx. Clasped hands earrings of hollow silver—single earring shows same curved modeling (right).

JACQUES FATH In 1948 couturier and glamour god Jacques Fath created jewelry with a secret: a pearl-covered ball ornament dangling from a pearl clip or necklace. Inside the ornament, which could be unscrewed into two hollow pieces, was a ball of cotton saturated with scent.

BUTTON, BUTTON The humble button was back in the spotlight during the 1940s, and there was a mighty good reason for its popularity: in 1947 a whopping 20 percent federal tax was imposed on costume jewelry. Gals thirsty for fashion but hungry for funds got around the tax by making their own jewelry—from buttons. "Buttons," wrote *Notions and Novelty Review* in 1942, "give home-mades the spark of the couturier." These weren't just ordinary buttons, but little treasures, embellished with cartoony themes, as on the "blue-plate special" button, which featured a doll-sized serving of meat loaf and mashed potatoes. Buttons could also be stitched together on a band of elastic to form a bracelet, or sewn on a ribbon to make a necklace.

Thanks to the president of the United States, the Scotty dog became a national mascot. President Roosevelt's pet captured popular fancy, and Scotties—in every size and shape, singly or in pairs—were immortalized in costume jewelry. This particular dog brooch was probably made at home by a hobbyist.

RHINESTONED SUNGLASSES Another of Hollywood's glamorous gifts to the world of fashion: rhinestoned plastic sunglasses. Costume jeweler Bee Norton was credited with this 1947 innovation, a design milestone that ranks with the decorated cigarette case.

THE DUCHESS OF WINDSOR Ever the trendsetter, the duchess provided toney inspiration for fine and costume jewelry alike during the 1930s and 1940. She wore a Cartier flamingo brooch, blazing with calibré-cut emeralds, rubies, and sapphires, on New Year's Day in 1941—the day that she arrived in the United States after her marriage to the duke. The flamingo was instantly made up in plastics and a variety of less-than-genuine materials, and it became one of the most popular and long-lived animal motifs in jewelry.

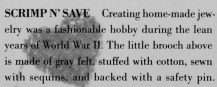

Direct costume copies were also made from the duchess's gold charm bracelet, hung with nine crosses, each inscribed with an intimate message from the duke on the back.

SCRIMP N' SAVE Creating home-made jewelry was a fashionable hobby during the lean years of World War II. The little brooch above is made of gray felt, stuffed with cotton, sewn with sequins, and backed with a safety pin.

As an indicator of the jewelry pinch, rhinestones, beads, and pearls were in such short supply that jewelers would literally buy them off a woman's back. Ladies would sell their lavish gem-embroidered sweaters, evening dresses, and stage costumes just for the decorations. Stripped from the dress, the gemstones were recycled into costume jewelry.

The shortage of gems and pearls encouraged peculiar behavior. One of the best-known costume pearl jewelers put a cloak and dagger operation into effect, depositing its entire inventory of fake pearls into bank vaults under the Empire State Building for safekeeping. When the pearls were needed, company executives visited the vault with a fleet of wheelbarrows to make a withdrawal.

A more elegant version of the wartime make-do attitude was the tufted sequin shoulder ornament by Arpad Necessories.

Witty Schiaparelli created perfume pins to fasten on a lapel. Her 1940 "Scamp" was a miniature wire dressmaker's body, shaped like a female torso, that held a glass flacon of her "Shocking" perfume. Another version was a tiny figure of a fencer, complete with sword, also concealing a perfume bottle. Prices in the late 1940s? $7.50.

JOSEFF OF HOLLYWOOD There really was a Joseff, and he really worked in Hollywood, designing the faux jewels seen in major motion pictures of the 1930s and 1940s. His credits include Loretta Young's parure in the film *Suez*, Bette Davis's royal jewels in *The Private Lives of Elizabeth and Essex*, and Greta Garbo's romantic gems in *Camille*. His first commercially available jewelry was sold during the 1950s.

Page 109: anything goes—and well together—
in the 1980s. The jewelry mix includes Happy
Face watch (1970s), coral cuff, signed "Miriam
Haskell" (1940s), copper bracelet, signed
"Renoir" (1950s), and cut-out bracelet, signed
"Bill Smith of Richilieu" (1970s). Page 110:
fantastical colored wooden-bead necklace,
earrings, and gravity-defying sculptural neck
ornament (worn in the hair) from the mid-
1960s, designed and made by Jules van Rouge.
Page 111: a pop bouquet from the 1960s,
featuring metal and enamel flower brooches and
a daisy-chain belt (worn as a necklace). Page
112: snowball-sized mottled green plastic beads
made a barbaric-style necklace from the 1930s.
Page 113: armload of bracelets hand-assembled
from miniature pearls and glass beads, signed
"Miriam Haskell," show the designer's signature
style from the 1930s and 1940s. Page 114: a
playful humor and casual technique (gems are
set with glue) mark bracelets, brooches, and
gloves heaped with fiery stones, signed "Wendy
Gell," as 1980s pieces. Page 115: opulent,
multiple-strand Oriental-style necklace of plastic
beads and rhinestone roundels, dating from the
late 1950s. Pages 116-117: a retrospective
sampling, signed "Chanel," of this grande
dame's faux jewels from the 1930s, 1940s, and
1950s. Page 118: gold-metal sea urchin brooch
from the late 1950s, signed "Original by
Robert," holds a spill of baroque pearls and
rhinestones. Page 119: huge colored stones make
a spectacular bib necklace from the 1960s, by
Jacques Libuono. Page 120: elaborate rhinestone
and pearl necklaces from the 1950s, signed
"Trifari." Page 121: beautiful, back-slung pearl
drapery, in the style of the 1920s. Pages 122-
123: fragile wreath necklace of glass posies and
baroque pearls from the 1930s, signed "Chanel."
Page 124: ultra-modern innovation from the 1970s
—plastic ring, signed "Cadoro," set with a single
rhinestone.

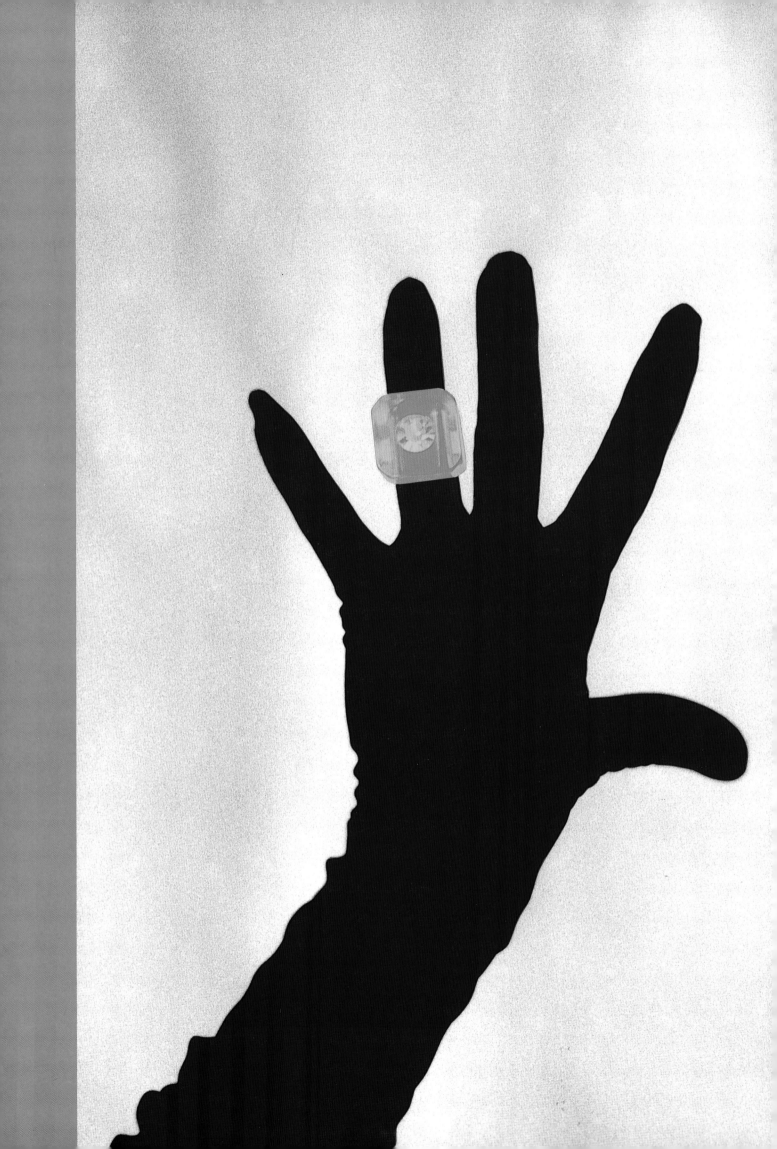

50's

Although the 1950s have been labeled the time of the "don't-rock-the-boat" status quo, fashion wasn't positioned so conservatively or comfortably. Marked by controversy, fashion maneuvered hemlines up and down and manipulated dress shapes from the bouffant to the balloon to the deflated baggy chemise. Suits were sculpted from stiff tweeds; at the same time clingy silk knits and jerseys permeated clothing styles. Costume jewelry's range was just as wide: neat bangles and charm bracelets of gold metal coexisted with elaborate bibs of monster-sized rhinestones.

It's surprising that such lavish extremism flourished during the era of President Eisenhower. By most accounts, he ruled over a complacent population: *Harper's Bazaar* called it "the unlost generation." The details of that definition: "They are settling down to jobs sooner, marrying earlier, and having more babies than their parents did." As popular cliché has it, those married women with babies were buttoned into car coats, station wagons, and suburbia. Sensible, they wore tweeds and unremarkable jewelry—a circle pin, a link bracelet. *Vogue* dubbed the typical woman of 1954 "Mrs. A.," and described her. "Mrs. A. (and she's a composite of a hundred women of our acquaintance) has been having-her-cake-and-eating-it ever since the move to the country, just after the second baby came along. . . . A weekday is as likely to find Mrs. A. lunching at a smart city restaurant as driving the new puppies down to the vet's for shots; an evening may mean a gala theatre opening—or an old Carole Lombard movie shown on the new projector to a living-roomful of friends (the rage of the A.'s countryside at the moment: rented films)."

Dressed for those evenings, "Mrs. A." and her opposite—the career girl—

Rhinestone bib necklace tipped with baroque glass emerald and ruby drops (opposite page), typical of the dramatic return to luxury after World War II. Earrings—a mix of smoky gray, topaz, and white rhinestones—complete the ensemble, signed "Napier." Necklace by Elsa Schiaparelli (center) defined 1950s glamour, while polka dots and button earrings (above) exemplified the decade's perkier, more innocent side.

BIG RINGS The bigger the ring, the better. Super-sized rings were fashion's make-believe for grownups. *Women's Wear Daily* trumpeted the reason behind its popularity in 1951, "Evenings at home, and home entertaining bring the hands into full focus, and the sleek, often trouser lounging fashions cry for the bold, gay stroke rings provide."

Too extreme to pass for genuine, the big ring had a chunky confidence. Its jewels were large, and its metal was flashy. The dome- or bombé-shaped ring was a best-seller. Its raised, curved surface was covered either with large lumps of faux stones and pearls, or smaller pavé-set rhinestones. The simply set, single gigantic stone was also a favorite. A variation was the all-metal bombé-shaped ring, its golden metal treated to give it a gravelly textured surface.

A peek at Miss America's jewelry trousseau (above), designed for her by Napier. Quintessential tailored jewelry set (opposite page)—earrings and a short necklace—made up in textured, brushed metal.

dazzled. The chic get-up of the 1950s was slightly sinister: false eyelashes, knife-sharp stiletto heels, and stockings stenciled with a leopard pattern were its emblems. A few other wardrobe choices, circa 1954, included "dinner suits and coats of gilt-embroidered paisley. Turbans of feathers, or of heavy striped silks. Oyster-white coats dripping with lynx. Printed satin dinner dresses in *boiserie* designs . . . Evening trench coats of gold-brocaded velvet." Thus garbed, this drop-dead glamour queen weighed herself down with chandelier earrings and masses of throat-clutching beads.

Where the femme fatale and the suburban woman came together was over a casserole. Entertaining, 1950s-style, was centered around the new technological wonder—the television set—and consisted of "evenings of Canasta, conversation and dinner-built-around-a-casserole." In cities and suburban subdivisions, these soirées represented a revolutionary concept of hospitality, and fashion and jewelry styles evolved to accommodate this new informal way of living well.

Italy and America came to the rescue most successfully, perhaps because casual wear was not a Parisian forté. A standard casual ensemble was the Italian-inspired uniform of black turtleneck sweater, cropped black Capri pants, and ballet flats (or sexy, slingback, high-heeled sandals) later seen on Audrey Hepburn, whom *Harper's Bazaar* credited with bringing the "Portofino look" to America. The jewelry that went with this look took the form of a glittering Oriental bib necklace or gold hoop earrings and as many metal bangles as the wearer dared brandish. This was a fashion first: sports and casual wear worn with elaborate jewelry.

Role models to emulate were movie stars such as Grace Kelly, Audrey Hepburn, and, late in the decade, the simple, fashion-editor style of Jackie Kennedy. The voluptuous, sex-symbol types — actresses Marilyn Monroe, Brigitte Bardot, Sophia Loren, and Elizabeth Taylor—had their followers too.

Both categories of female type could find costume jewelry to suit their styles. Oriental-style jewelry was the glamorous queen; last seen in the 1940s, it came back as V-shaped jeweled bib necklaces, humongous chandelier drop earrings, and wide jeweled bracelets. Total fakery, this movie-star quality jewelry didn't even attempt to look real.

Every bit its majestic equal was Chanel-inspired Renaissance jewelry, which remained in vogue well into the 1960s. Or, one could look to a revival of the Edwardian style, recognizable as the dog collar. The collar's scale was a match for the Oriental bibs, making use of the same big stones, and big pearls, made up into multiple-strand collars. The jewelry worked well with the bare, low-cut bodices of Edwardian-influenced dresses and with the new baggy "sack" dress, which covered every part of the body except the neck.

The temperamental opposites of these styles were tailored costume jewelry and neat little novelties. Tasteful, predictable, this jewelry was also versatile, worn in a low-key style (a circle pin, a single gold hoop bracelet, one flower pin),

or with its own brand of extravagance (for example, charm bracelets and bangles worn in a clanking mass, from wrist to elbow). Made of silver or gold metal, tailored jewelry was also host to a major innovation: the introduction of texture. Jewelry was brushed, dented, chiseled, and roughed up, an echo of new developments in fashionable fabrics.

Beads were versatile in the same way, tidily brought to life by couturier Christian Dior in the early 1950s. By the end of the decade, they'd grown wild, and came in a mix of exaggerated sizes, worn in a thick jumble around neck and wrist.

Behind this change in jewelry's makeup was a change in fashion's silhouettes. The chemise, the sheath, the trapeze, and the sack were popular dress shapes; they shared narrow skirts and a bagginess that only offered a hint of the female form. With these loose dresses, all emphasis fell squarely on the only exposed body parts: legs, wrist, neck, and head. Just to stay visible, costume jewelry increased its scale to bold-sized: wide chokers, giant bib necklaces, and bracelets worn in profusion (hairdos turned massive for the same reason— balance).

Clothing color wasn't shy, either. "It was a timid woman who did not have something mauve, gypsy pink, orange or blazing red in her wardrobe," said the *New York Times*, analyzing the decade in 1959. The flip side: muted tones for day, as set out by *Harper's Bazaar*, "misty slate, deep charcoal, every conceivable, curious color of brown, olive-bronze, greens, mustard, mulberry." Plastic and glass beads were every bit the match for these murky tones, made up in a rainbow of intense colors and innovative treatments (speckled, dashed, and dotted with color, much like tweed fabric). Iridescent color was created in the mid-1950s, and rhinestones and beads (as well as the sequins on those fabulous 1950s sweaters) were touched with its transparent shimmer of color.

For the first time since the early 1930s, white jewelry was worn. Balenciaga introduced white to fashion in 1953, and the blizzard of white continued throughout the decade. Ultra-chic, white was usually found on plastic or enamel pieces, and it crossed all style boundaries, from the simple (the single strand of beads) to the more elaborate (the heavily beaded bib necklace and bunchy bracelet).

The versatility of 1950s costume jewelry—its innovative pairing of formal jewelry with casual clothing—set the stage for the 1960s, when distinctions between "daytime" and "evening" jewelry blurred. Although fashion and the feminine ideal changed radically, there was a less dramatic break between the jewelry of the 1950s and 1960s than there had been between earlier decades. In some cases, jewelry didn't alter from the 1950s to the 1960s at all; notable examples were the Oriental bib necklace, the chandelier earring, and the big ring. Perhaps the period also sowed the seeds of coming revolution, as 1950s jewelry designs became less strict in their obedience to the dictates of Paris, turning instead to the more relaxed American and Italian looks.

ORIENTAL LUXURY

The perfect neck and shoulders for the Oriental-style necklace belonged to actress Audrey Hepburn: her swan neck provided a dramatic balance for that weighty mass of jewelry. Hepburn's elongated body and gamine face was one of the feminine ideals of the period, and this exotic jewelry was another 1950s standard.

It was jewelry that blazed with light. Bib necklaces and collars were composed of giant sparkling rhinestones. Drop earrings shook with tiers of pearls and faceted stones. Bracelets were on fire, often blinding, colossal three-inch-wide ornaments. Jewels were even worn in the hair, tucked into stiff, upswept coiffures. This was a royal drench of jewels, fit for America's new fashion queens.

"The fashionable way wends East this fall," prophesied the *New York Times* in 1955, "through caftan coats and harem drapery, rich brocades and mandarin sheaths. But the quickest way to Oriental chic is a thick paving of pseudo-Eastern jewelry atop a simple costume. Western jewelry designers have discovered the Orient and have copied its fabled treasures at less than fabulous prices." Originally patterned after the precious jewelry of India's royalty, the Oriental (or "East Indian") style retained every bit of its lavish heritage. Roots for the Oriental/East Indian revival of the 1950s can be traced back to the end of the 1940s, when rhinestones and artificial pearls could once again be used for costume jewelry. The availability of these materials—coupled with the passion for ultrafeminine fashions after the war—contributed to the popularity of an elaborate style.

Couturiers Christian Dior and Jacques Fath, who rose to fashionable prominence about the same time, were the creative forces behind these spectacular accessories. In 1947 Dior had launched mega-sized jeweled collars and chokers to accompany the full skirts of his romantic "New Look," which was the definition of "female" after the war and on into the 1950s. Fath attracted attention for his similarly spectacular jewelry, even designing a special line of pearl costume jewelry for the American Marvella company.

Oriental jewelry wasn't restricted to elaborate rhinestone and pearl confections. There were also replicas of authentic Middle Eastern jewelry, made up in gold and silver: necklaces and bracelets rattled with temple bells, beads, spikes, coins, tassels, and stylized flowers. Hoop earrings and "slave bracelets" for the upper arm were even more exotic fashionable accessories.

The Oriental bib was the most popular jewelry silhouette of the 1950s, neck-and-neck with the rope of beads and/or pearls. Necklaces were flat-lying, flexible collars, or V-shaped bibs, built with beads, pearls, cut stones, cabochons—single or in combination. Clasps were simple, usually a hook-and-eye, or discreetly hidden in the collar itself. Added flash was given by a fringe of pearls, rhinestones, or beads edging the necklace. Late in the decade, the flat bib necklace mutated into a tumbled, "semi-bib" style. The ornaments were still centered in front like a bib, but they were jumbled into a bulky heap of different-sized jewels and beads, rather than lying flat.

Necklaces, earrings, and bracelets alike were made up in a free-for-all assortment of materials, set in gold or silver metal. Startling new combinations included pearls mixed with rubies, jet with crystal, emeralds with turquoise and rubies, and rhinestones with beads and pearls. A pearl called the "peanut," a great, elongated baroque drop, was a common element used by Paris couture jewelers, beginning in 1956.

Jewelry color itself was a technicolor fairy tale: the "peacock" combination of faux emeralds and sapphires was a specifically 1950s innovation. Transparent faceted stones were color-matched by cabochons, beads, and pearls (both plain and baroque) in smoky gray, pale brown, and a brown topaz. Another notable ingredient was the iridescent stone, the "aurora borealis," available for the first time in the summer of 1956. The aurora borealis gave a shimmering rainbow color to both clear and transparent colored beads and stones. Size and texture became newly important and stones grew to the size of almonds, olives, and crab apples.

Jewelry's new palette complemented the wave of stylish colors unleashed by fashion: mauve, blue, and lavender, peridot green, yellow, and gray were its fresh, soft tones. However, this rainbow wasn't the only story for clothing, and the "little black dress" remained a favorite—also a complement for jewel colors.

Around 1954, promoted by couturier Balenciaga, white made its debut. It became a fashion standard—a bleached version of basic black—and jewelry paled along with it. No jewelry material took to white as well as plastic, and plastic bib necklaces, collars, and bracelets were all popular.

Couturier Balenciaga featured a lavish gold-metal and glass-bead necklace (opposite page, above) in his fall 1954 collection. Another dazzler (right), a flexible bib of smoke-colored rhinestones, is edged with baroque pearls. The longest strand is six inches. Variations of the Oriental necklace in plastic (opposite page). Plastic—especially white plastic—was wildly popular.

The silhouette of the 1950s clothing was simple—but that's what made this elaborate jewelry work so well. "Counterbalancing the sharp, pure line, the disciplined composure that's what's best about the best American clothes, there's this," instructed *Harper's Bazaar* in 1955, "happening all around you, a flash and jingle of jewels. Heavy wristloads of them. Massed ropes of them. Big, bold dazzlers, lighting up the scene." Fashion had rebounded from the war in glory, baring the bosom, the neck, the shoulders, and most of the back. These necklines scooped, plunged, were cut in a deep V, or bateau shape, framing the cascade of jeweled bib necklaces. Dresses were cut low in back, too, generously exposing skin. The backless style was perfect for the collar necklaces, the circle of their jewels expanding around front and back.

The bib necklace was versatile—just as dazzling worn with the opposite of the bare look: the turtleneck sweater. The turtleneck was glamorous, associated with Italian fashions, and the beatniks. Its severe silhouette and solid color made a dramatic background for displaying these necklaces.

Besides jewelry, there were also direct fashion steals from India, including dresses cut from original antique saris (started by the Duchess of Windsor in the late 1940s). Dior showed gauze gold sari scarves. The "hostess gown" found its niche as more and more entertaining was done at home. Inspired by the Middle East and India, the harem look had hostesses clad in gauzy loose trousers with overskirts, skinny legged pajamas with fringe, and floor-length caftans. Even when it wasn't an "Indian-style" outfit, Paris used Indian metallic fabrics and rich brocades for evening wear. The exotic reigned on Broadway, too: *The King and I* and *Kismet* featured Eastern-inspired costumes and accessories.

When the Oriental style originally became part of costume jewelry's vocabulary in the 1930s, it was mostly limited to gold metal or polished semi-precious beads (no flashy cut stones). In contrast, the elaborate Oriental jewelry of the 1950s and late 1940s was characterized by a dramatic, almost cinematic excess. The rougher, more authentic quality of the 1930s style (gold metal, Buddha beads, etc.) appears almost dull in comparison. While the jewelry's basic format remained the same, the somber stones and metal of the earlier pieces were exchanged for a showy Hollywood dazzle in the 1950s incarnation.

ROMANCING HISTORY

Pomp and circumstance came to life with the coronation of Queen Elizabeth II in 1952. Anything associated with royalty was of immense interest. Fashion happily obliged this interest, offering costume jewelry fit for kings or queens, its motifs copied from treasures of the Renaissance and Edwardian periods. Even the queen's little sister, Princess Margaret, was also something of a trendsetter for the younger set. A smattering of influences from royalty of other periods, notably that of Marie Antoinette of France, also showed up in jewelry.

The Renaissance Look

In reviving the treasures of Queen Elizabeth I and King Henry VIII some centuries later, costume jewelry kept their unrestrained magnificence, re-interpreting baroque pearls, gold settings, and round and square precious cut stones. In the Renaissance style, stones were set roughly, to look as if they were embedded or poured into gold metal while it was still soft. The stones themselves were usually uncut, incorporated as a dull color accent, and lumpish and irregular in shape. Colorful enamelwork added an extra fillip of richness. Costume jewelry also adopted the Renaissance's goliath-sized link chains, with and without pendants (medallions, crosses, or figures of imaginary creatures), as well as its brooches—circular or oval three-dimensional domes, built up with stones and pearls, or made up in the girandole format, with a classic threesome of hanging stones or pearls.

The Renaissance revival in costume jewelry was supported by none other than Coco Chanel, who had had an early fascination with England. In the spring of 1957 she offered Renaissance accessories: a gold Maltese cross set with pearls on a hefty gold chain; big, cross-shaped brooches, and long pearl and gold-chain sautoirs. Chanel even had the mannequins in her show wear her costume jewelry in a manner copied straight from the Renaissance: necklaces were looped over the bodice and pinned on one shoulder with a brooch. This sumptuous, gem-heavy jewelry became most recognizable as the "Chanel" style, surviving even into the 1960s. As always, what Chanel started was picked up by other costume jewelry companies who copied her copies, although sometimes with less lavish results.

Massive Renaissance jewelry was a rich contrast—and a wonderful complement—to the clothing it accessorized in the 1950s. Fuss, frills, and trim-

A jumble of amber and yellow lightweight plastic beads (opposite page, above) made up a hefty necklace. The Oriental style of late-1950s jewelry continued well into the 1960s; Brooch and earrings (opposite page center) of turquoise plastic and rhinestones set in gold metal, signed "Trifari." Revamped Renaissance brooches and a cross pendant (this page) made of poured glass and baroque pearls set in tarnished gold metal, all signed "Chanel."

ming had vanished at the hands of the decade's master designers, Balenciaga and Dior, who preached the importance of pure line: the sharp silhouette of their clothes was a striking contrast to the solid Renaissance jewelry. The easy modernity of Chanel's ensembles worked in the same way with her jewelry. Chanel's neat suits, worn with a crisp white blouse with turned-back cuffs, were a perfect foil for the weight of gold and stones. The jewelry also provided a humorous contrast between the original, rather primitive king's ransom of riches and its modern translation into glass and base metal.

The Edwardian Style

In 1956 *My Fair Lady* opened on Broadway, starring Cecil Beaton's costumes. True to the period in which the play was set (early 1900s), Beaton created fancy, Edwardian-flavored outfits, featuring Empire waists, cartwheel hats, and parasols. Long a popular figure with the fashion magazines, Beaton was extolled and his costumes were lavishly photographed, praised, and touted as style-setting designs.

The pearl choker necklace was the most notable Edwardian-era jewelry steal. Originally the tight-fitting, multiple-strand choker was associated with Queen Alexandria of England, who made it her personal "look," hiding a not-so-beautiful neck at the same time. In the 1950s the choker was championed by

Heavy pendant in the Renaissance style (above), measuring two-and-a-half inches across, is made of dark-toned poured glass and a drop baroque pearl (signed "Chanel"). Ropes of baroque pearls and glass ornaments (left). Classic rope of pearls worn choker style (right).

couturiers Christian Dior and Jacques Fath, and in 1957 both featured chokers in their fashion collections. These trailblazing versions added extravagance to the original pearls, mixing in jet glass beads, balls of iridescent stones, and giant-sized rhinestones. For those women blessed with a swan-like neck, chokers could be worn three at a time, with a flat-collar or bib necklace added for extra dazzle.

By the end of the 1950s the choker had infiltrated casual cothing as well as evening wear, creating sophisticated, yet informal ensembles for at-home entertaining, the decade's national pastime. Elaborate jewels worn with sweaters and slacks made fashion news, blurring all boundaries between proper "evening" and "daytime" jewelry. In 1959 *Life* magazine photographed Elizabeth Taylor in a black jet Dior choker, worn with a low-cut black sweater.

The choker was also the perfect accessory for one of the ruling dress silhouettes of the day: the sack. Literally like its name, the "sack" completely hid the body in its baggy folds. In a conversation with Dior, the master of the sack dress, Chanel exclaimed, "You dress women like armchairs!" Since the neck was the only limb bared by the sack, the choker was the logical—the only—style choice for costume jewelry. Any jewelry hanging over the dress would have broken the line of the garment.

When Dior died unexpectedly in 1957 his youthful successor, Yves St. Laurent, launched his first solo collection with the trapeze dress. While his dress had a new shape, St. Laurent didn't alter Dior's pioneering jewelry, but kept the same Edwardian-style chokers. An eyewitness at St. Laurent's 1959 show reported, "Yves St. Laurent at Dior rediscovers the charm of Edwardian chokers which he combines with matching necklaces—all magnificently made of jet, pearls, or brilliants with huge jewels nestled here and there below the hollow of the neck, among the many, many necklace strands."

Marie Antoinette also cast her long shadow into revival fashions. The French jewelry firm Gripoix (responsible for much of the Paris couturier costume jewelry for the past three decades) was inspired by an exhibition of artifacts related to Marie Antoinette at Versailles in 1953. The company's jewelry collection of that year featured variations on the French queen's favorite jewelry motifs, most notably the girandole earring. This earring style, associated with both Queen Marie and the Empress Eugénie, was a 1950s fashion standard for evening wear. This decade did its version in a flashy, dazzling, oversized manner, with its hanging ornament extending nearly to the shoulder. Earrings also came in the chandelier format, clusters and falls of mixed stones and pearls. These earrings had a jittery mobility—practically the only thing that could move on the fashionable heads of the day, with their coiffures stiffly lacquered with hair spray or covered with pinned-down false hairpieces.

Yves St. Laurent, designing for Dior, accessorized his 1959 couture collection with massive chokers (left).

TAILORED JEWELRY

Tailored jewelry is the stuff of 1950s legend. Simple, straightforward modern metal jewelry, it indulged in no romantic flights of fancy and few razzle-dazzle stones. Tailored jewelry was distinguished by its flatness and a lack of ornate detailing. The only dose of drama occurred when it was worn against black clothing or en masse. As a style, it was primarily associated with Italian sportswear and the casual American attitude. (The French tastemakers preferred to accessorize their couture with cut stones and beads.) Its roll call included the tasteful—if unexciting—gold bangle bracelet; the nice—if unexceptional—gold hoop earring. Gold was the most prevalent color, in a bright or dull finish. Tarnished antique gold, called "Edwardian" in this decade (in the 1940s it was known as "Victorian"), was also common. Silver metal, created by rhodium plating, took second place in popularity.

Tailored jewelry was an interesting species. It could be stylishly flamboyant for sophisticated at-home entertaining. *Life* magazine spelled out the details, "To go with the stylishly casual at-home clothes that grew up around tv . . . bracelets by the dozen now burden arms, earrings come as big as ears permit, and necklaces are worn waist-deep." Worn in less profusion, it went to the office and

Tailored earrings (above) show traces of 1940s design influences. Metal tassels fancy up a silver necklace (left), signed "Monet." Necklace and bracelet set (opposite page) have the stiff, simple shapes and shiny finish typical of early 1950s jewelry (signed "Napier").

the supermarket. With white gloves still very much part of a lady's ensemble, the well-behaved bracelet was parked just above the cuff. In the evening, gloves were tossed off, and a more dramatic mix of bangles and chains, stacked from wrist to elbow, was donned. That versatility made the tailored type a unique classic and prompted *Life* to remark again, "Too much jewelry on the street is now scarcely enough at home." This clanking bracelet armor was the black sheep of the tailored jewelry family. Its only equivalent was the jumble of glass and plastic bead necklaces the fashionables massed by the half dozen around their necks.

Tailored jewelry had its richest play with bracelets. There were large and small, link, mesh, snake chain, and plain bangle bracelets. A flourish of chain fringe was a frequent feature. Chain bracelets might hold coins, toy-like charms, tiny pearls, and the occasional chunk of metal. These wrist rattlers weren't cheap: in 1952, the stylish bracelet was in the fairly pricy range of $2.34 to $23.50 each.

Flower brooch of lightweight gold metal mesh, is five inches across. In the 1950s, it would have been pinned on the shoulder, the center of a bodice, or at the waist.

Earrings were a 1950s focal point, for the simple reason that women's ears showed. Hair was worn short, or maneuvered back into a ponytail, or teased into an ear-baring poof or chignon. Both earrings and brooches were variations of the same shapes: the spiky spray, the dome, the "atomic" snow flake of the 1940s, the circle pin, and the hoop earring. Hoop earrings could be fat, skinny, oversized, small, plain or studded with tiny stones and pearls.

The most innovative aspect of tailored jewelry was its new textured surface—a look lifted from fabric. Costume and precious jewelry mimicked the roughness of bulky tweeds and knits, slubbed and ribbed silks and linens, even fabrics woven with reindeer fur. Fashion magazines did their bit to alert the stylish to this development. *Vogue* sent up the smoke signal in 1954, in an article entitled "American Accessories: A Complete Reshuffle." It explained, "Golden opportunities in accessories: the new textured gilt jewelry—replicas in metal of linen, embroidery, and wicker." Favorite textured finishes were "Florentine" (brushed to look like overlaid scratches) and "satin" (a mat surface). Words like "chiseled" and "nubby" were used to describe these rugged metal treatments. Texture continued to be part of the costume jewelry vocabulary well into the 1960s.

Close-up look at costume jewelry's new rough-textured metal surface (above).

NOVELTY JEWELRY

This was the decade novelty jewelry lost some of its punch. The chic, surrealistic humor that had marked the 1930s novelties, or the make-do whimsy of the 1940s jewelry, went nowhere in the 1950s. There was little slapstick jewelry this time around; the "cute" accessory was re-defined. Even the queen of fashion humor, Elsa Schiaparelli, lost her stylish giggle: her costume jewelry from this period was pretty, safe, and lacked the innovative appeal that had characterized her earlier work.

It was as if that touch of mink—the suburban status symbol—had replaced that touch of mirth. The ladies of the best-dressed list—Audrey Hepburn, Grace Kelly, Marlene Dietrich, Babe Paley, Mrs. William Guest—were a fairly somber group, without the giddy, personal flamboyance that had been the trademark of the trendsetters of the 1920s and 1930s, such as Daisy Fellowes and Mrs. Harrison Williams. The 1950s absolutely shrank from the kind of loud display championed by earlier novelty jewelry. One little poodle pin, a few scattered flower brooches, and a wristful of charms were all the accessory impact this decade craved. Unlike earlier eras, there were no "novelty" necklaces, hung with poodle charms, for example, in the manner of the vintage necklaces.

The poodle pin, shown in gold metal (above), was a 1950s mascot. Jeweled animals and flowers (right) are signed "Trifari."

For fans only (above): the official rock n' roll Elvis Presley ankle bracelet. Designer Claire McCardell put American sportswear on the map. For three to four years, she also made costume jewelry, available in a handful of stores. Evidence of her art (below)—a lapel pin made of gold metal, spinning a chunky glass globe. Unfortunately none of her jewelry was signed; this pin still boasts its red-and-gold paper tag. Chunky bracelet (opposite page) jangles silver-metal and plastic charms (signed "Napier"). Blooming-with-jewels brooches: a brushed gold-metal flower edged with tiny rhinestones; the bloom below it boasts invisibly set red stones and leaves sparkling with rhinestones; a tiny turtle is topped with a shellful of stones (all signed "Trifari").

In the 1950s, the charm bracelet carried the banner for novelty jewelry almost single-handedly. Jingling, jangling, and burdened with a bone-crunching array of charms, it was popular with women of all ages and fashion persuasions.

The bracelet itself was usually a large-linked, flexible metal chain; variations included pearls or cut-stone chains. Customarily, the charms were made out of the same metal as the chain from which they dangled; they were also made up in glass and plastic. Ornaments for these bracelets ranged from tiny detailed figures, studded with a few tasteful gems or pearls, to rough lumps of stones and beads. Slightly enlarged, charms could also have been worn as brooches.

More than just decoration, charms were an avidly collected, sentimental passion. The more embellishment the bracelet boasted, the more heft it commanded, the better. The bracelet was also a democratic accessory. Plentiful and cheap, most charms were priced below $2.00, so there were charms for everyone. Noted the *Jeweler's Circular* in 1956, "Both the farm lady and the First Lady wore charms." The First Lady was Mamie Eisenhower, who never made the best-dressed list. Charms did make it on everyone's personal list, however; teens wore the bracelets; so did their mothers and their big sisters. Symptomatic of the psyche of the time, the best-selling charm was the baby bootie. Telephones and cars were popular also; the only items missing from the ranks of domestic souvenirs were the washer and dryer. Poodles—the favorite 1950s pet and fashion motif—were often found kenneled on the charm bracelet.

Individual charms could be purchased to commemorate occasions such as a birthday, anniversary, graduation, Mother's Day, or receipt of a first driver's license, or they could be accumulated through travel. GI's often visited the countries where they had been stationed during the war and would return with gifts of charms depicting the Eiffel Tower, or the Leaning Tower of Pisa. As more and more families could afford to take vacations, women bought their own charms too.

Jewelry companies helped those collectors by offering pre-assembled charm bracelets, usually organized around a theme, for example, Oriental, which heavily influenced the fashions of the 1950s through culture as well as through less lofty sources (the hit film *Love Is a Many Splendored Thing* and the play *The King and I* on Broadway were both set in the Orient). Oriental charms included Chinese characters inscribed on plaques, the seated Buddha, fish, good-luck coins, bits of coral and turquoise, pagodas, dragons, temple dancers, and Oriental faces. These same elements found their way onto other jewelry items, incorporated as design motifs.

This era doted on articulated charms. There were bird cages with tiny birds rattling inside, baby grand pianos with liftable lids, padlocks that really locked with a tiny key. More useful for the harried housewife were miniature pillbox charms that opened to hold a few pills. It was interesting—and probably not co-incidental—that these handy pillboxes were created about the time tranquilizers and stimulants came into use (the infamous Benzedrine and Dexedrine). "Pills to keep you going and pills to slow you down were increasingly regarded as standard equipment for vest pockets and purse-size pillboxes," was the report from *Harper's Bazaar* in 1959, reflecting on the decade.

Along with charms, flower jewelry filled the 1950s novelty garden. It may seem like a stretch of the imagination, but the coronation of Queen Elizabeth II of England in 1952 planted the flower in fashion. According to the *New York Times*, "Because all eyes are on England this year, English gardens will have a share in the picture . . . huge sprays of rhinestones suggest stylized roses, daisies, and the French fleur de lis. Tinted enamel, combined with pearls and semiprecious stones, make clusters of violets, pansies, bluets, and lilies of the valley for boutonnieres and lapels. Embossed or sculpted in gold, many flower shapes are joined together for necklaces and bracelets, and mounted as pins." In 1957 Dior created rhinestone daisies; Chanel was responsible for a floral wreath necklace, made up of silver metal flowers. The flower remained a motif throughout the period, fabricated in a wild variety of materials and styles; with and without jewels, in metal, plastic, or combinations of all three. Most notable was the flower pin, which could be a flat, stylized "sunburst" circle of petals, or a realistic bloom, both made up in metal and hand-tinted in clear enamel colors. The flower continued into the 1960s, when the daisy pin took on a vibrant new pop art color and fell under a new banner: "Flower Power."

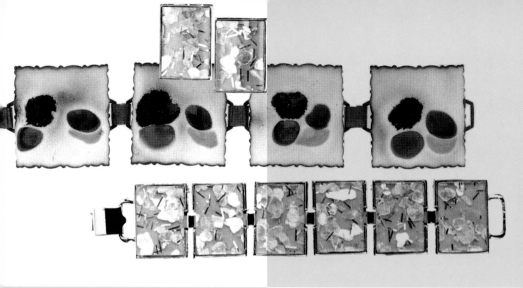

HOBBY JEWELRY Jewelry made by crafts enthusiasts in the fabulous '50s had its own distinctive mark. This sampler features a "modern-look" group of bracelets made of enameled copper and glitter set in clear plastic.

Lapel pins were still a big item. Above, a tiny bauble of poured glass hangs from a bar pin. Inside there's a cotton pad soaking up a bit of perfume.

The last decade to elaborately package costume jewelry in satin-lined boxes was the 1950s. This vintage set is by Trifari.

The lady who couldn't come up with the cash for a mink coat had a small consolation: mink earrings. In the mid 1950s these real fur button earrings clung to many ears, for only $3 a pair. The most popular version was made of white mink, followed by the champagne and brown varieties.

SPARKLING BELTS Set with giant brilliants, rhinestones, shells, and tiny figures, transparent plastic was shaped into twinkling belts in 1954. Handbags got into the act, too, but, oddly, the style of embedding three-dimensional objects in plastic did not cross over to jewelry.

For a fashion collection designed by Italy's Fontana Sisters, Napier created a "rosary-bead" and cross necklace, a style that would be revived in the 1980s.

President Eisenhower's name, set in rhinestones on a bracelet made of tiny pearls, made a jewelry conversation piece.

POP-IT BEADS Hollow plastic "pop" beads, which came in a rainbow of colors and could be snapped together to form necklaces and bracelets of any length, were popular with adult women as well as young girls. The jewelry could be broken apart and put back together again in an entirely different way when the wearer wanted a change.

SAKS FIFTH AVENUE

There was no such thing as "too much" or "too outrageous" in the 1960s. Boom years, the decade had so much money to fling around that absolutely anything would sell. Both fashion and jewelry crammed a whirlwind of different looks into a brief space of time, as "precious," "pretty," and "small-scale" fell from grace as stylish descriptions.

In the slang of the period, fashion was "switched on" to the young. "The Old Guard no longer sets fashion . . . the mood is youth—youth—youth," was *Women's Wear Daily*'s tart observation. Youth took nothing at face value, or for granted. "Nobody ever looked like them before; they're the zingos who bolted the pack . . . crashed out of the mould and smashed it to smithereens . . . invented their own look, their own sound, their own age . . . knocked over the establishment and established themselves for today . . . " was *Vogue*'s crack analysis of 1965's young rebels. And Clairol's live-for-the-moment ad cried, "If I've only one life, let me live it as a blonde!"

Coupled with youth, thinness, as exemplified by the little girl-like Twiggy, was the way to go. "The new leg is a little girl leg," reported the Herald Tribune, " . . . to be stuck with legs and calves is just too crass for words . . . legs and arms seem to match, as they do with a child."

Besides the androgynous Twiggy, the old femininity was threatened by the many-headed Hydra of rock n' roll, unisex fashions, drugs, and a female liberation propelled by the Pill. "One of our national concerns today is that women are losing their femininity . . . " crabbed the *Ladies' Home Journal*, " . . . you can't tell today's teenage girl about boys, of course, but even she is better than her bewigged older sister in the fashion magazines. You can't tell her *from* the boys."

This decade loved larger-than-life jewelry: here; a flexible, supersized earring and a ring spanning a hand's width (left), hand-assembled of silver plastic and pearls, by Jules van Rouge; four-inch-wide decked bracelet with rock-sized stones (above), by Jacques Libuono.

Gender confusion was just part of the picture. For all its emphasis on youth, and the tyranny of the new, this was a haunted decade. Man made it to the moon—and returned to a scarred planet, troubled by assassinations, riots, the Vietnam War, civil rights unrest.

In such a feverish climate, fashion had a temporal quality. There was a haste, a black humor in fragile clothing and jewelry made of plastic, sequins, or paper. Celebrated for the shortness of its lifespan, fashion wasn't made to last— a fitting epitaph for the 1960s.

The ideal girl of the 1960s was an Amazon. She was impossibly tall, skinny, with hair impossibly puffed and padded into a balloon; she had an impossibly arrogant fashion attitude. Her micro-mini skirts and dresses, small enough to be no-account, were worn over legs patterned with wild stockings. For the first time, makeup and jewelry were put on by the pound. Amazons brandished gigantic fake eyelashes, thick pale eyeshadow, thick pale lipstick, body bronzer, painted-on freckles. With it all went jewelry that went beyond extreme to the point of self parody: colossal plastic necklaces that looked like a bonfire around the neck and shoulders, iceberg rings, snowball earrings, gladiator cuff bracelets.

The high-fashion ideal was just one of the many looks creating a dizzy spiral of changing styles that gave rise to adjectives such as "Rocket Age," "Tough Chic," "Orbit," and the "LSD school." And that spiral had costume jewelry in a quick-change frenzy.

"Modern" was shorthand for fashion's changes; "mod" was even shorter. Mods wore utterly simple, streamlined clothes that had their own kind of aggression. In Paris, couturiers Cardin, Courrèges, Ungaro, and Rabanne were the architects of the style. In London, the mods had designer Mary Quant. Revolution and rebellion was symbolized by the mini, "the classic design of our time," according to Quant, its creator. The uncomplication of this clothing was part of its charm and youthfulness. Action words fit them, "zip up, pop on, and just go——zing! . . . no hooks, no ties . . . everything clings, swings, ready to orbit . . ."

Indicative of the climate of change, the fashion hierarchy was revolutionized as well. Couture didn't wear the same crown. Wearing an "original" lost cachet. "Fashion has ceased to be the prerogative of the rich," observed Yves St. Laurent, "the office girl, the girl in the factory, can now follow fashion movements almost with the same ease and often with more conviction than the duchess . . . couturier, haute couture, la mode—they're all terms that are passé." Yves St. Laurent was one of the first to sell ready-made clothes. Earlier, Mary Quant claimed, "There was a time when clothes were a sure sign of a woman's position and income group. Not now. Snobbery has gone out of style and in our shops you will find duchesses jostling with typists to buy the same dresses."

This couture downscale was paralleled in costume jewelry: it was hip for the rich and fashionable to flaunt fake jewelry. American costume jeweler Kenneth Jay Lane introduced his versions of the exclusive Cartier and David Webb jew-

Jewelry still life (above): brooches and necklaces, as arranged in Harper's Bazaar *in 1961. The wide collar necklace of plastic or glass beads, by Napier, (opposite page, left) was a 1950s look that remained popular through the 1960s. A modern counterpoint (opposite page, right): bunchy metal bracelets and huge earring, by Cadoro. Pierced, hollow-ball earrings (opposite page, below) typified the popular Oriental style of ornament, signed "Monet."*

elry, and socialites and secretaries vied with each other for it over the jewelry counter. Dress for the clubs (Arthur, Cheetah, The Dom, Yellowfinger) wasn't diamonds—it was crazy, larger-than-life jewelry, bold enough to wear with the jungle-cat pyjamas, the harem pants, the Pucci prints, and the sequinned mini-dresses.

Women (and, for the first time, men) could take their pick of role models. The era's first goddess was Jackie Kennedy. The lesson she gave America was, ". . . the simplicity of fashion-editor taste . . . . Her little nothing dresses, her unadorned cloth coats, her plain pillboxes and pumps had been upper-crust specialities. They became mass fads." Pearls were the proper accessory with this look. At the other end of the style spectrum were the rough clads of the counter culture. Hipster stars Sonny and Cher were described from a fashion magazine point of view in 1965, "Sonny's lionheart haircut, his knee-length buckskin boots, his possum and bobcat jackets. Cher's waterfall of dense black hair, her pale deep-eyed radiance, her hundred pairs of below-navel, belled pants. (Nineteen-year-old Cher doesn't own a dress.)" There were socialites, foreign princesses, the luminaries of the best-dressed list. The movies also cast a stylish shadow: the four B's were *Barbarella, Bonnie and Clyde, James Bond, Blow-Up*. Other fashion-affecting notables included models: The Twig (Twiggy), The Shrimp (Jean Shrimpton), and the towering Verushka. Fashion magazines piled lush fantasies on their readers, ushering them from an African safari to a sultan's palace in India, to outer space.

Closer to home, England was the jewel in fashion's crown. "Every era has its favorite capital and its final price; the gay Nineties in Berlin; the Forties in Hollywood; La Dolce Vita Fifties in Rome. And the Sixties, at least for a little while, belonged to London," recorded *Goodbye Baby & Amen*, the scrapbook of the era. Among the multitudes of pop groups, the Beatles and Rolling Stones had their clothes, baubles, haircuts, and conversation copied by hordes of fans—men and women.

The costume jewelry that sold ran the gamut from the handmade-looking counter-culture variety, with its emphasis on humble materials (beads, yarn, temple bells, leather), to the voluptuous gold chunks of Renaissance-look jewelry. Between these two types lay the splendor of the Oriental style, with gems stolen from Cleopatra or characters out of Arabian fairy tales, and the bright, confident, hard-edged shapes of "mod" jewelry, done in futuristic plastics and metal. For the less courageous, there was jewelry of the serviceable tailored variety—slight metal chain necklaces and bracelets, worn with tiny, irritating pairs of novelty animal pins (poodles, cats, etc.). Pieces that could be best decribed as fantasy jewelry were emblematic of the decade, their raw materials a mind-expanding, unlikely assortment of raffia, cork, plastic and papier mâché, feathers and cardboard. But whatever "costume" it might don, costume jewelry of the 1960s was inspired by Peter Pan—ephemeral, eternally young, and more than a little bit make-believe.

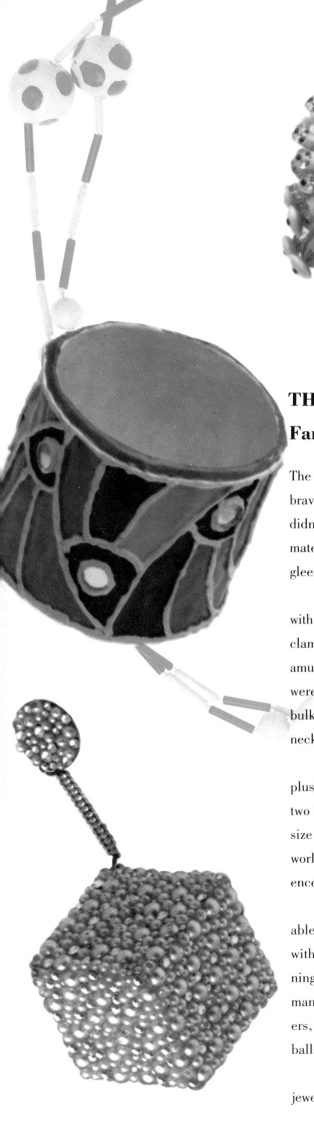

THE WILD STYLE
Fantasy Jewelry

The 1960s excelled at excess, and fantasy jewelry was made to order. Fearless bravado and a good dose of "let's pretend" were its chief attributes. This jewelry didn't have a single "look": its only unifying feature was its use of innovative materials, from the ludicrous to the fabulous, put together in an untraditional, gleefully disrespectful way.

Familiar jewelry styles—Indian bib collars, pendant earrings—were hit with a hallucinatory dash of make-believe. Jewelry was blown up to a huge scale; clamoring pop colors and clashing patterns were standard. Materials were amusing, flimsy, impractical, improvised, and splendidly outrageous. There were towering headdresses and hair ornaments built up from pearls and beads; bulky, gravity-defying icicle earrings; loopy bracelets bristling with ornaments; necklaces of snowball-sized beads.

Magazines featured the extraordinary model Verushka, her body (six feet plus) decked in superhuman-scale doodads. Plastic blocks, each one the size of two ice cubes, dangled from her ears. On her fingers she wore plastic rings the size of golf balls. Awkwardly ebullient, like fashion, jewelry took on an otherworldly, escapist quality. It didn't matter that most women didn't have the presence to carry off exaggerated jewelry: theater was for everyone.

As part of its theatrical nature, jewelry worn for "day" was indistinguishable from that worn for "evening." New-Age jewelry was made of pop materials with a showy, temporal quality. Materials originally intended for handbags, evening dresses, and crafts projects (pearls, sequins, beads, plastic pieces) were manipulated into novel creations. Other jewelry ingredients included feathers, wood, papier-mâché, cork, Christmas tinsel, cardboard, tassels, styrofoam balls, raffia, vinyl, suede, and fake hairpieces in brilliant colors.

The very way these materials were put together created a whole new type of jewelry. To make the jewelry flexible and lightweight (to compensate for its large

Fantasy play (opposite page, top to bottom): monster bracelet of plastic beads (by Arpad Necessories); hand-painted, four-inch-wide papier-mâché cuff decorated with inset mirrors (by Bill Smith); polka-dot necklace of papier-mâché balls; gargantuan, four-inch-wide hollow cube earring; and chunky bracelet covered with rhinestones (by Arpad Necessories). Glass beads strung on flexible wire (above) could be manipulated to different lengths and widths. Head-to-shoulder feather earrings (inset, above), worn with a pair of big-as-golf-ball rings (by Jules van Rouge).

size), the pieces were threaded on thin wire, or sewn, glued, or tied together. It was up to the artist's ingenuity to get the pieces to work.

The solutions were inventive: silvery plastic linked disks became a showery necklace. An ostrich feather, or a pink silk tassel, was worn at the ears. Wrists were swallowed by huge rows of beads, or thick papier-mâché cuffs dotted with faux jewels. Unlikely combinations worked: cork with pearls, suede with plastic, vinyl with rhinestones.

This wasn't perfectly made jewelry—but it wasn't trying to be. *Vogue* put a notable fantasy necklace in the spotlight in 1965, "Over the shoulder, a load of jewelry that's fascinating, new—looks like chunks of chewing gum embedded with bits of mirror, painted with black and white designs in papier-mâché."

Some of this monster-sized jewelry had a unique problem: it was nearly too

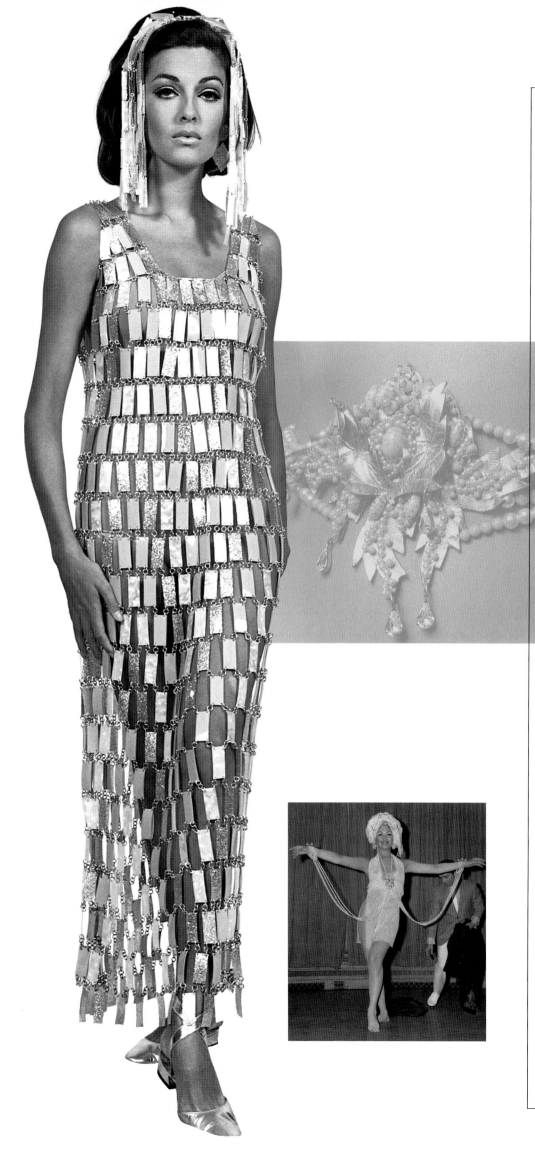

BODY JEWELRY   A new body consciousness was born in the Age of Aquarius. Not only did more body show, it was shown off in new ways. The definition of what was "clothing" and what was "jewelry" was pushed to new limits. Sometimes, the two were made of the same materials. The working formula could have been: make a necklace longer and it's a dress.

In New York, high-fashion costume jewelry artists Jules van Rouge, Cadoro, Lee Menichetti, and Giorgio di Sant' Angelo turned out ornaments for the body. Bras, breastplates, and halter tops were made from a wild assortment of materials. There were halter tops of medieval-looking leather studded with nailheads, metal mesh, white leather embroidered with rhinestones, stone-studded metal, and chains. Pearls and beads were woven into headdresses, vests, and mini-dresses. Clanking, rattling dresses made of plastic links looked as if they needed a can opener to get into. Women could dress like mod Apaches in strips of jeweled and woven leather, or like disco visitors from outer space in silver plastic links fashioned into a loose bib that reached the waist. The shy wore body jewelry over body stockings; the bold wore it over a transparent shirt—or over bare skin, as uncomfortable as it might have been.

New York was first to create body jewelry, but Paris wasn't far behind. In Paris, Paco Rabanne was one of the best known body jewelry innovators. Rabanne used pliers and wires to hinge together circles and squares of plastic into garments.

In the spring of 1969, Yves St. Laurent unveiled his version of body jewelry: he had model Verushka's bust and midriff molded in metal by sculptor Claude Lelanne. On the runway, his mannequin wore the Verushka metal breasts with a long skirt and was greeted with applause. "This way every woman can have a figure for see-through and body revealing clothes," was *Women's Wear Daily*'s common-sensical review. The *New York Times* was even more practical, noting that body jewelry was "meant for young, modest-sized bosoms, and apparently the effect is worth the somewhat cold feeling of metal against skin."

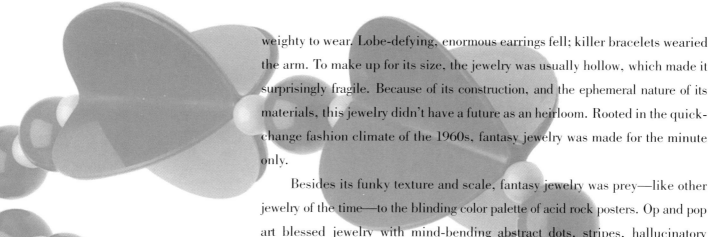

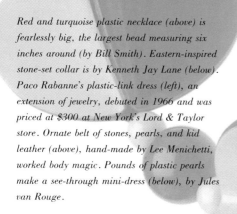

Red and turquoise plastic necklace (above) is fearlessly big, the largest bead measuring six inches around (by Bill Smith). Eastern-inspired stone-set collar is by Kenneth Jay Lane (below). Paco Rabanne's plastic-link dress (left), an extension of jewelry, debuted in 1966 and was priced at $300 at New York's Lord & Taylor store. Ornate belt of stones, pearls, and kid leather (above), hand-made by Lee Menichetti, worked body magic. Pounds of plastic pearls make a see-through mini-dress (below), by Jules van Rouge.

weighty to wear. Lobe-defying, enormous earrings fell; killer bracelets wearied the arm. To make up for its size, the jewelry was usually hollow, which made it surprisingly fragile. Because of its construction, and the ephemeral nature of its materials, this jewelry didn't have a future as an heirloom. Rooted in the quick-change fashion climate of the 1960s, fantasy jewelry was made for the minute only.

Besides its funky texture and scale, fantasy jewelry was prey—like other jewelry of the time—to the blinding color palette of acid rock posters. Op and pop art blessed jewelry with mind-bending abstract dots, stripes, hallucinatory squiggles, the bull's eye, spirals, checks, and arrows, all done up in hot pink with orange and green, yellow and purple, black and white. Silvery, moonstruck, shiny metallics were also popular, especially because of their ability to reflect light. Light bounced off baubles set with hundreds of cut stones, plastic discs, and tiny mirrors, which attracted attention—a major part of the jewelry's appeal.

Along with its light-show characteristics, fantasy jewelry was made to-move. Earrings were long and mobile; trembling trim shook on bracelets and necklaces. Even in the hair, jewelry quivered. This swinging jewelry was all put to motion with women's mini-skirted strides and the jerky wiggle of dances like the Swim and the Frug.

Fantasy jewelry was made by hand by a new breed of designer, who may or may not have had jewelry training. The innovative materials used for these pieces didn't require a jeweler's knowledge or technique. Intricate, hand-assembled, and often hand-painted, this jewelry was often impossible to manufacture on a major scale, although it was made, in a more toned-down, simplified version, by large mass-market jewelry companies.

Fantasy jewelry designers didn't follow Paris—theirs was American-inspired jewelry. Rocking with bravado, these showy baubles populated the pages of the major fashion magazines, and many spectacular pieces were specially made just for a magazine's photo session. *Vogue's* editor-in-chief during the 1960s, Diana Vreeland, was a supporter of the extravagant look, and she filled the magazine with an eye-boggling array of commissioned fantasy jewelry.

When fantasy jewelry was available, it was sold primarily in boutiques. One jewelry designer recalls the long line of hopeful artisans and hippie craftsmen camped out with their samples in front of the Henri Bendel store in New York City on the days the shop reviewed new jewelry.

These singular accessories set a direction for mass-market jewelry and were much copied. In a climate in which showing the latest outrageous fashion was all-important, this jewelry had its own niche. Fantasy jewelry was to inspire, to awe, to entertain—it wasn't necessarily for all women to wear in real life. It was a pure fashion expression.

Existing now only in the pages of fashion magazines, this wildly amazing form of ornament occupies a unique spot in the story of style. With fantasy jewelry, costume jewelry reached the ultimate "costume" of its definition.

Counter-culture Jewelry

In 1965 *Vogue* magazine ran a feature on shopping for second-hand clothes—not just any second-hand clothing, but army surplus gear, workshirts, and jeans. From a hippie counter-culture emblem, this clothing became a credible fashion "look" for women and men. In protest the *New York Times* scolded, "Surely few Americans who grew up during the Depression . . . would have dreamed that, by 1967, some of their most gifted sons and daughters would purposely be hurrying from riches to rags."

Counter-culture clothing was splendid and sometimes sloppy. In addition to the dressed-down standards, there were ponchos, djellabahs, dashikis, and ethnic caftans. Strictly personal decorations included studs, fringe, beads, and a variety of appliqués, embroidery, and patches (portraying the American flag and the peace symbol, for example). The costume jewelry that accompanied this wardrobe was just as unconventional, symbolic, and worn by both sexes. Prized for what it represented, rather than for its value or beauty, this was costume jewelry with its own rough appeal and a "hang easy" attitude. Necklaces—"love beads"—casually made of papier-mâché, clay, wood, or glass, were favored front runners. They could also be made of feathers, bells, rope, yarn, or string. This "back to nature" choice of materials also affected mass-market costume jewelry, which adopted the use of leather, fabric, and papier-mâché.

In the 1960s, men took a turn at playing peacock. One example: a gold-metal link necklace with a Greek head pendant, worn with aplomb (signed "Monet"). Signs of the times (above): a Gemini symbol pendant and a silver-metal peace symbol (center), both customarily worn on a thin strip of suede leather.

MEN'S JEWELRY Fashion-conscious men tossed aside neckties in favor of necklaces. With that action, the man on the street joined the ranks of hipster style revolutionaries like Richard Burton and the Earl of Snowdon. In 1968 the earl wore a gold eagle on a gold chain, plus a copper wrist bangle. Pierre Cardin offered aluminum and silver pendant necklaces set with uncut diamonds for $1,000. In the costume jewelry line, there were necklaces for men dangling disks, bells, abstract shapes, crosses with enamel and fake stones, zodiac symbols and the peace sign, and heraldics. Hippies put ceramic or ivory beads on a ribbon, string, or strip of leather.

The style philosophy was expressed by a Gimbel's store ad in 1968, "Men . . . planning a getaway weekend? Pack a turtle, a Nehru, and don't get caught without a smart shining something around your liberated neck. It's what's happening in leisure wear . . . " How'd the "shining something" look? In the slang of the era, "outta sight, man."

The necklace was standard equipment for male rock n' rollers and movie stars, hippies, and jet set fashion upstarts, a symbol of their more advanced and sensitive states. To wear a necklace was to make a counter-cultural gesture. It was a gesture that wasn't accepted everywhere. Sniped the *New York Times*, "The hippie clanking around in his beads and bells should be having the last laugh—his necklace is becoming an uptown 'thing.' " Men had to overcome prejudice to put themselves in necklace chains. It wasn't always easy; sometimes it was even forbidden. Tiffany's was a case in point. Announced the president of Tiffany's in 1968, "If we know a man is buying a necklace for himself, we will refuse to sell it."

In Hollywood, home of the hip, masculine jewelry was embraced. "I don't think beads are effeminate," said actor George Hamilton, who wore a dangling jade heart and beads . . . "they're putting masculinity back in balance."

The interest in Eastern religions, and increased jet travel, made exotic jewelry from Africa, the Middle East, India, Tibet, and Native American Indian sources popular. The "Black is Beautiful" movement also created an appreciation and awareness of ethnic African jewelry. This imported jewelry was available in "head shops" and hippie boutiques in most cities. Its natural ingredients included ivory, bone, amber, wood, and ceramics. Silver was the metal with the right feeling; metal filigree bracelets, earrings, and necklaces tinkled with tiny bells, charms, and amulets. Singer Janis Joplin made ethnic jewelry her signature: she covered both arms, wrist to elbow, with silver bangles. Both men and women pierced their ears (and sometimes their nostrils) to wear hoop rings.

Massive hand-made sterling silver bracelet (above), with a spiral hinge, measures five inches wide (signed Susan Kelner Freeman); peace symbol pendant (below) in the form of a streamlined dove, made of aluminum. Animated jewelry was a specialty of the era. Playful pachyderm pendant (opposite page, right) has a head that wiggles and a rhinestone body (by Jacques Libuono); jointed gold-metal jumping clown (opposite page, upper right) hangs from a necklace; variation of the Happy Face (opposite page, lower right): a gold-metal pin with wandering rhinestone eyes.

The anguish and fallout of the Vietnam War provided a dark background to the decade. The cheap second-hand and ethnic clothing and the valueless jewelry were all part of the war protest movement. During World War II, women had been proud to "wear poor"—with make-do clothing, and costume jewelry of ad-libbed materials such as felt, leather, and shells. However, because the Vietnam War was not generally supported, the 1960s did not give rise to soldier pins, red, white, and blue pieces, or charm bracelets hung with hand grenades and bombers the way the 1940s had. Instead of sentimental jewelry, buttons expressed the prevalent—often opposing—feelings.

Buttons expressed sentiment in shorthand: "America: love it or leave it," "Make love not war," "Hell no, we won't go." In terms of design, this type of "jewelry" consisted of little more than the same bold graphics found on posters, protest banners, and graffiti. Subjects included the peace and love symbols, the ankh (the sign of life), the yin and yang, the clenched fist representing "black power," and the signs of the zodiac.

Late in the 1960s, at the height of the Vietnam War, P.O.W. ID bracelets, inscribed with a missing serviceman's name and date, were worn as a memento of protest until he was found. Not quite in the fashion mainstream, counter-culture jewelry made a statement that remains a part of fashion history.

POP NOVELTIES

The flowery, fluttery sensibility of youth was everywhere. The daisy—the prettiest, least politically provocative emblem of the younger generation—found its way into posters, tattoos, and bumper stickers, and fashion took it to heart. It appeared on "threads" from blue jeans to couture. In 1967, *Harper's Bazaar* made note of the year's hit, "The patterned fur coat, a must with colored fur flowers . . . "

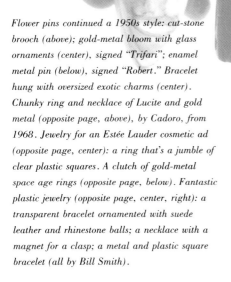

Flower power was just one notable novelty motif: Other jewelry subjects were taken from the animal ark, from frogs to kittens. Animals and flowers were important for both costume and precious jewelry. Virtually identical, their designs fall into two distinct groups: the rich, colorful work of precious jeweler David Webb, and the flat, poster/cartoon school. Webb and Cartier sparked the craze for Renaissance jewelry, distinguished by its bright enamel colors, baroque pearls, and colorful cut stones—all copied in costume jewelry. To the Renaissance vocabulary of mythological beasts and men, novelty jewelry added a menagerie of cutesy animals: poodles, turtles, butterflies. Copy in a CoroCraft ad in 1965 read, "If they fly, flutter, or float, they flatter . . . gilded creatures with bright jeweled eyes, their natural habitat is a bare lapel or a deserted stretch of neckline." The ad featured a gold turtle, a lizard, and a bee pin. These creatures were modeled in 3-D, set with stones or painted with enamel; they also came in plain metal, with a heavy, rough texture. Some of the same animals— particularly the snake, the ram, and the lizard—became bracelets. These small ornaments continued the scatter pin tradition started in the late 1940s.

The flower sprouted up as a pop art-inspired, flat-as-a-pancake brooch, or as a more real-looking, relief-modeled bloom. Pop style novelty flowers looked as if they were lifted straight from a poster: flat, and flat-painted with bright colors, they were made up in everything from metal to plastic to papier-mâché. The most common shape was the daisy—a circle surrounded by a thicket of petals, sometimes set on a stalk. It came in psychedelic shades—orange paired with hot pink, lime with fuchsia, day glow yellow with cerise, or black with white— and was a dazzling accessory, worn on the multi-patterned fabrics (checks, stripes, tweedy and paisley mixes) that made up the 1960s wardrobe spectrum.

The stars of couture—Dior, Chanel, Givenchy, Ricci—did their versions of the jeweled flower, too. Their beautiful brooches set with cut stones and enamel paint followed a simple, straightforward design, creating elegantly "with it" versions of flower power.

The novelty jewelry of the 1960s had a stiff, stilted quality: the animals were awkward, the flowers were frozen. Humor, the hallmark of the novelty motif, seemed to be channeled into the making of theatrical fantasy jewelry, where it made a bigger splash. The novelty style had become a safe, conservative choice, an evolution begun in the 1950s.

Flower pins continued a 1950s style: cut-stone brooch (above); gold-metal bloom with glass ornaments (center), signed "Trifari"; enamel metal pin (below), signed "Robert." Bracelet hung with oversized exotic charms (center). Chunky ring and necklace of Lucite and gold metal (opposite page, above), by Cadoro, from 1968. Jewelry for an Estée Lauder cosmetic ad (opposite page, center): a ring that's a jumble of clear plastic squares. A clutch of gold-metal space age rings (opposite page, below). Fantastic plastic jewelry (opposite page, center, right): a transparent bracelet ornamented with suede leather and rhinestone balls; a necklace with a magnet for a clasp; a metal and plastic square bracelet (all by Bill Smith).

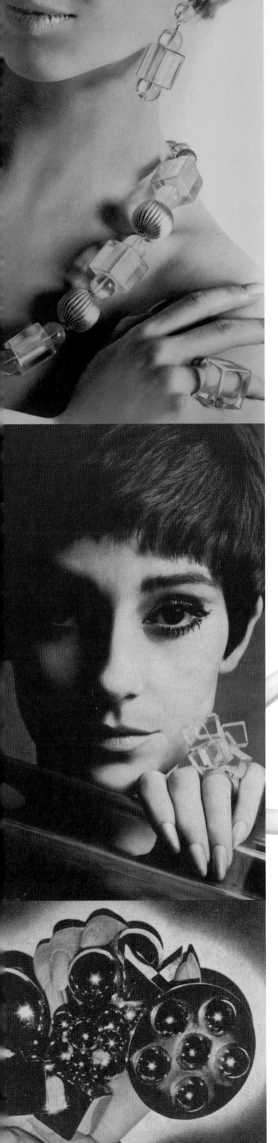

THE MOD LOOK

Man's walk on the moon sprinkled stardust on the 1960s, putting the vocabulary of that space trip on everyone's lips. A black dress was described as "intergalactic." According to fashion magazine copy, shoes were "space crafted" in "silver rocket" colors, and there were "new wools in fashion's orbit." Models posed at the NASA launch pad in futuristic fashions that could have been cooked up in Dr. No's laboratory.

Couturier Courrèges, one of the godfathers of the space-age style, had his showroom staffers display the look: ". . . brisk, bizarre young women with short hair, blinking through white spectacles, little white boots at the end of their athletic legs and stark white triangles of dresses skimming their skinny hips . . . " These goddesses looked for all the world like villainesses from a science-fiction comic book.

The jewelry worn by these alien princesses was as stiff and uncompromising as their clothes. Couturier Ungaro offered a sampling of the modern jewelry styles, ". . . aluminum necklaces-cum-bras teamed with aluminum hip-belts on see-through flower-appliquéd trousers. There was once a transparent silver-gray cape covered with tiny metal cylinders, and on another occasion a group of futuristic, metal, evening fantasies: one a gilded metal birdcage and matching metal skirt worn by a bare-breasted girl." This jewelry was simple, oversized, geometric. Materials were usually silver or gold metal, with a rocket-smooth surface. A jewelry magazine described the look in 1966, "The space-age love of geometric forms . . . cubes, triangles, circles and squares dangled as shoulder-length earrings, twined around wrists and shot out on pins." Plastic—especially transparent, pale-tinted, or white plastic—was a mod-look favorite.

Plastic sampler (above): clear tubular brooch set with rhinestones, and cylinders, squares, and balls of transparent tinted plastic to wear on the hand (all by Bill Smith). Heavy, gem-studded cuffs and brooch (below), by Kenneth Jay Lane. Playful mermaids, dragons, and other fanciful creatures incarnated as brooches, signed "Trifari." Chanel masterpiece (opposite page, center): a brooch of rich red and green poured glass.

Plastic was also a part of other fashions: platform shoes had three-inch transparent plastic heels, purses had transparent plastic chain handles, and there were eyeglasses, hats, and raincoats of see-through plastic.

Jewelry appeared as huge, shaped collars of metal that swooped across the shoulders, metal waist clinchers, and bracelets that imprisoned the wrist in a six-inch stretch of smooth silver. Another aspect of this modern jewelry was that when overgrown, it became body jewelry. A metal necklace held up a dress, a harness necklace became a halter top.

The early modern jewelry of the mid-1960s grew into the industrial motif of the latter part of the decade. Couturier Pierre Cardin introduced the giant industrial zipper to fashion, and Yves St. Laurent featured dresses studded with nailheads. Hinges replaced buttons; buckles held up straps. Caps, boots, handbags, vests, and skirts bristled with spikes and grommets. The chain was a popular motif, featured on shoes, gloves—even bikini-top straps. In costume jewelry, this hardware showed up as the belt, a top accessory in 1967. Belts rode low on jumpsuits, elongated sweaters, skinny ribbed dresses, knit pants, lean tunics—the uniform looks. St. Laurent made the classic chain belt the best-seller of the day: a series of simple linked metal circles, hooked in front, made of metal, or plastic "tortoise," were priced at $9 each. Belts were also done in elaborate jeweled Oriental and Renaissance styles.

By 1969, the industrial jewelry trend was so prevalent that Bloomingdale's in New York City opened a jewelry and belt boutique called the Foundry. Fashion columnist Eugenia Shepard packed a time capsule for *Harper's Bazaar* in 1967. Inside, she wrote, would be stowed "a lot of jingling brass hardware and . . . at least one chain belt and an industrial zipper."

RENAISSANCE UPDATE

Whose voices were heard in the land in 1968? 'Twas Romeo and his teen love, Juliet. Franco Zefferelli's movie of Shakespeare's romantic duo found an audience of real-life counterparts. Men wore flowing poet shirts; women favored a trailing Pre-Raphaelite look featuring high-waisted velvet dresses and long loose hair in crimped waves or ringlets. As seen in the film and on the street—with a boost from couture—the accompanying Renaissance-style jewelry was heavy and voluptuous.

In the 1960s, Renaissance jewelry was created by fine and costume jewelers alike, vamped, exaggerated, and worn with the flamboyance that characterized the period. Necklaces and bracelets were stacked, and rhinestones, turquoise, and coral-colored stones were added. The era also gave the style a slightly psy-

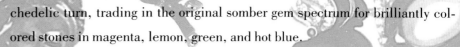

chedelic turn, trading in the original somber gem spectrum for brilliantly colored stones in magenta, lemon, green, and hot blue.

Prestige for the wealthy was a wrist-to-elbow armload of enamel and stone animal bracelets by Cartier and David Webb, priced from $3,500 to $10,000 each. The wealthy weren't above sneaking in a few imitations of these fabulous bracelets, however. Costume jewelry designer Kenneth Jay Lane cheerfully editioned faux versions, priced at a discreet $50 per bracelet in 1966. Both jewelry types depicted mythological and real creatures, such as a snarling tiger, with pavé stones, coiled around the wrist with his tail in his mouth, modeled in jeweled 3-D.

Crosses—Renaissance and otherwise—were in their element in the mystical 1960s. The cross later made a crossover and became a fashion item, minus the original funky attitude. "In the Age of Aquarius, the cross is becoming a high fashion symbol," reported the *New York Times* in 1969. "Crosses—big, bold and often hung as multiples in assorted shapes and sizes are being worn by mannequins, socialities and other stylish pacesetters." Gloria Vanderbilt had a cross made of jet and rhinestones measuring six inches. Fashion designer Halston had a Maltese cross, worn on a strip of red suede. Said he, "People are wearing crosses because they don't wear diamonds now . . . I'm not a jewelry nut, but I think the cross is such a sweet idea."

Although many couturiers and costume jewelers put their names to Renaissance-style gems, none did it as consistently as Coco Chanel. Since the 1950s, she had made these pieces her jewelry "Cadillac," showing crosses with her powdery pale tweed suits. In the late 1960s, Broadway launched a play about Chanel's life, starring Katharine Hepburn, which brought Renaissance jewelry back into the fashion limelight. The cross was a Chanel jewelry classic, studded with faux emeralds, rhinestones and rubies, big stones, and baroque pearls hung on a heavy chain or worn as a brooch, true to the original Renaissance models. Byzantine, Maltese, Greek, and Latin crosses were also part of the vocabulary.

This rich, ponderous jewelry, the stuff of history, stood in curious juxtaposition to the spare, space-age fashion of Cardin and Courrèges. In 1965, Yves St. Laurent launched his modern Mondrian-patterned dresses. *Women's Wear Daily* as there for the collection, reporting on the jewelry worn with the Mondrians: ". . . . the square brooch looks medieval and is very modern at the same time." The only "modern" thing about this jewelry was its neat setting, a cleaned-up version of the almost-gooey looking Renaissance setting, and it looked slightly jarring with the simple, geometric clothes. St. Laurent's square cross brooch had geometrically cut faux topaz, rubies, emeralds, plus pearls, and it was worn pinned just below the shoulder of the dress.

Given the à go-go temperament of the 1960s, it was surprising that the rich Renaissance style was embraced. But the decade has also been billed as one of the most romantic, and elaborate fashions were nothing if not romantic.

INFLUENCES FROM THE EAST

The mid-1960s scene at discos and parties looked like a casting call for a James Bond movie set in the Middle East, with women dressed like a cross between an Egyptian princess and a go-go dancer. Even Jackie Kennedy, after her marriage to Aristotle Onassis, was sighted in a Schéhérazade-style outfit: a vest sewn with gold coins, worn with loose harem trousers. Billowy silk chalwar pants, embroidered djellabahs, fluid caftans, harem jumpsuits, paisley brocade Nehru suits, and sumptuous lamé sheath dresses—jeweled at the neck and hem—all topped off with fake hairpieces, jeweled headdresses, and theatrical make-up, completed the dress-up look.

Even in the age of the Youthquake and the first Pepsi generation, Cleopatra's charms still fascinated. Cleopatra—in the form of Elizabeth Taylor—made a comeback in the movie of the same name; the world was captivated by the Taylor/Richard Burton romance on the film set. And Egypt stayed in the news when the pharaoh's ancient temples were moved for the building of the Aswan Dam. The Egyptian appeal widened to include India—the focus of new interest when the Beatles journeyed there to meet a guru, followed by hordes of pilgrims, hippies, and others.

Eastern-influenced costume jewelry jingled right along—a rich riot of gem-decked bibs, chandelier earrings, heavy bangles, and ornamental versions of the asp, drawn from Egyptian, East Indian, and Moroccan sources. Lavish decoration and generous size were hallmarks of these pieces, which featured odd combinations that took historical and geographic liberties—an Indian bib might be set with scarabs or a ponderous gold-metal necklace might have East Indian or Mayan motifs. The jewelry was comic-book colorful: cabochons in "Egyptian" salmon, pink, and turquoise; cut stones in every shade of the rainbow; tinted pearls; fireballs of mixed stones. Bright gold was the "ancient" metal of choice.

Even couture in Paris was infected with an exotic fever. Although Coco Chanel had snorted, ". . . fashion cannot come up from the street; it can only go down into the street," in 1967 she caved in and borrowed from the "street's" hippie passion for Middle Eastern and North African jewelry to produce intricate,

Tiered, sculpted metal earring (right) just tickles the shoulder (signed "Napier"). Elaborate metal pendant (above) worn as an earring—just for effect. Jeweled sandals (center) set with rhinestones, faux rubies, and sapphires were a 1966 bit of flashy exoticism, as shown in Harper's Bazaar *with body paint à la Goldfinger and frosted gold and silver polish on toenails.*

Pair of twisted metal bracelets (opposite page, above) matched with a pinky ring. Yves St. Laurent's imaginative necklace (opposite page, left) shown with one of his couture collections. Lavish stone-set, gold-metal pin, five-and-a-half inches wide, by Jacques Libuono.

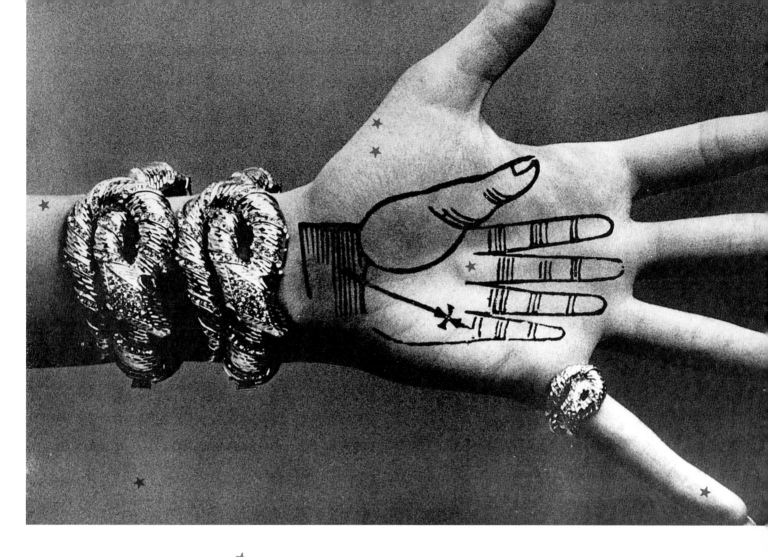

filigreed pieces. (The "street" had been wearing North African jewelry years before Chanel's version.) That gesture from the couture Establishment was just the beginning. Yves St. Laurent fell under the spell of Morocco in 1969, startling *Women's Wear Daily* by wearing his satin shirts unbuttoned to the waist. That year, his collection featured printed panne velvet outfits, trailing scarves, and chain belts clanking around the hips, worn with pants cut low enough for a belly dancer. Dior's 1965 collection featured elegant "Hindoustani" caftans and turbans, picked up by hostesses around the world. The caftan was a 1960s favorite—in couture as well as cheaper hippie versions. The caftan's simplicity made it the ideal background for a pile of necklaces.

A pillow on the floor was the decade's preferred form of seating, and bare feet were the mark of the casual caftaned hostess. Costume jewelry evolved with this approach, creating accessories for bare feet: a jeweled bracelet wound around the ankle, connected to a jeweled strap ending in a toe ring. In one of its more fanciful moments, *Vogue* even showed "Maharani mittens." The mitten was a jeweled contraption that stretched across the top of the hand, connecting a ring and a bracelet.

The 1960s were prosperous times, and Eastern-style jewelry and fashion echoed the vigor and exuberance of those years. Their lavishness was an escape, too, from the cataclysmic events that shadowed the period. This style created its own magical no-man's-land, a fairy tale for grown-ups where exotica flourished.

Toward the end of the 1960s the metal stud became a popular ornament, decorating jeans, jewelry—even leggings.

KENNETH JAY LANE The high priest of costume jewelry in the 1960s was Kenneth Jay Lane. Lane built up his jewelry business from ground level, starting with rhinestone shoe ornaments in 1963. His lavish fake gems caught the eye of fashion editors and the Beautiful People, who gleefully mixed their $30 "K.J.L." panther bracelets with similar ones set with genuine stones. Lane's studio on East 38th Street in New York City attracted a crowd of "ladies from the Social Register and the best-dressed lists [who] would turn up to help with sorting and shipping." The designer recalls, "On any given day…you might have found Babe Paley, Greta Garbo, two baronesses de Rothschild, three editors, six messengers, a cousin, four girl friends and their mothers, Andy Warhol and the Velvet Underground, two film stars, three film stars' wives, two girl friends' mothers' husbands buying for their girl friends." Even jewelry maven the Duchess of Windsor could have joined the throng: she owned a Lane belt covered in rhinestones.

The bejeweled panther has a fabulous history. The articulated Cartier version (above) was a special mascot of the firm since 1917, when it was first created. Later on, Cartier designer Jeanne Toussaint made panther jewelry for style setters such as heiress Barbara Hutton. The Duke of Windsor presented his wife with many gifts of jewelry with a panther motif from the 1940s through the 1960s. Faux-jewel panthers were designed by Kenneth Jay Lane

and became sought-after members of the costume jewlery menagerie.

The legendary Chanel was thrust into the spotlight in 1969, with the Broadway production of Coco, *based on the designer's life. Katharine Hepburn played the starring role. Coco's costumes and costume jewelry inspired the look of clothing and gems, such as seen in the original sketch by Cadoro (right) for their "Chanel" line.*

WIGGED-OUT HAIR

In the late eighteenth century Marie Antoinette wore towering hairdos padded with powdered hairpieces and decorated with jewels, flowers, ribbons—even tiny figurines and flags. Several centuries later the fashionables of the 1960s again gloried in exaggerated hair. *Vogue* described a beauty in 1966 who wore "a splendor of hair that's made full use of the hairpiece revolution and has obviously absorbed the entire afternoon of some hairdressing genius." *Vogue* added, "One thousand percent faked up, engineered from extended crown to lacquered toe, she is an Excitement."

Hair excitement was engineered by a handful of legendary coiffure artists. Fake hairpieces, braids, and switches were de rigueur, twisted and twined into astonishing sculptures and then stiffened with spray. Jeweled bobby pins, hair combs, and barrettes, as well as actual pieces of costume jewelry—brooches, earrings, lengths of pearls—were tucked, pinned, and draped among the curls, swirls, and braids.

WATCHES

In 1964, right in tune with the ticking tempo of the times, the mod watch was born. The big watch was unisex. Teens and hip older types could now wear "his" watch on "her" wrist. The basic format: an oversized watch face strapped to an oversized watch band. The watch came in many shapes; the bulky two- to three-inch straps were available in a variety of materials, colors, and patterns, including brocades, satin, printed fabric (paisley, psychedelics, geometrics), leather, textured metal, and plastic. Switchable watch bands were favored: a single watch face could be snapped off and on a wardrobe of these wild straps.

Ancestor to the mod watch was the pendant watch. Generally small in scale, pendant timepieces (round, oval, square, pear shape, hexagonal) hung at the end of a chain. Textures and materials were borrowed from the necklace counterpart—in fact, some ticking neckwear was indistinguishable from the purely ornamental necklace.

O's

AND CHANEL AGAIN AS "COCO"

DRAWING BOARD

#4375E $500
BLACK/PRL
GOLD/PRL

#6464P.
GOLD/RS./PRL.
AS WORN BY MISS
KATHERINE HEPBURN
IN "COCO"

A

After the exuberant, dress-to-excess thunder of the 1960s, with its flowered vinyl mini-skirts and Cleopatra-scaled jewels, style in the 1970s sounded a bleat of bewilderment. Fashion was floundering; teetering wildly from one extreme to another, it embraced both Hot Pants and the businesswoman's floppy bowtie in the same decade. Casualness and a growing conservatism were hallmarks of the era, brightened by the flash of disco dressing, the ubiquitous gold chain, and the seeds of punk rebellion in the latter half of the period.

No single style—or designer—emerged as the strong-armed leader of the 1970s. Paris showed outrageous, near-exhibitionist clothes, while New York (and America in general) came into its own with a simplified, comfortable wardrobe that could go to work. The mix of trends was an attempt to make up for the demise of high fashion, and magazines ran articles lamenting the death of couture. T-shirts and blue jeans were transformed into a full-fledged fashion fad, requiring the opposite of elegance in ornamentation—a thin gold chain, tiny gold earrings, and the physically fit good looks of the all-American girl next door, as embodied in the 1970s pin-up beauty, Farrah Fawcett-Majors, praised for her "down-to-earth accessible glamor."

A shrinking, "think small" attitude pervaded the fashionable look of the decade; its tone was set by the worst recession to occur in thirty years. *Time* magazine noted, "It became chic to cut back, and vulgar—as well as dangero-rus—to show off." In 1971 *Women's Wear Daily* deadpanned, "It's so chic not to

Jewelry punk-style (opposite page): grommets, spikes, and metal studs on leather were hallmarks of this fashion revolution. Streamlined, super-scaled, hand-made metal necklace collar (above), signed "Robert Lee Morris."

Chains and pendants were the most popular jewelry choice for both men and women in the 1970s. A he-man-sized gold-metal pendant hangs from a heavy chain (opposite page), signed "Napier." A fox graces a silver-metal pendant (above), worn as a reminder of an endangered species (signed "Napier"). Boots—a wardrobe staple of the decade—were sometimes even embellished with jeweled ornaments (center), signed "Cadoro."

look moneyed that two New York stores . . . recently opened denim clothing and accessories boutiques."

With fashion taking a down-played turn, costume jewelry weakly followed. One popular style comprised "ethnic" or "hand-crafted" baubles, a hangover from the anti-materialist, back-to-nature movement of the 1960s. Materials included wood, glass, ceramic beads, polished stones, seeds, feathers, coconut shards, shells, or smooth, polished plastic, wood, or metal shapes. These elements were woven together with macramé string or cord (more sophisticated designers used strips of suede or silk cord). Fashion magazines gave step-by-step directions for hand-knotting macramé jewelry, plant holders, place mats, and vests—all punctuated by rough beads and bits of wood. Another type of non-establishment influence, the "Black is Beautiful" movement, strengthened its hold on 1970s fashion, offering African-inspired materials for jewelry, such as amber, ivory, and wood.

Reflecting a new self-consciousness, and a less socially expansive spirit, the 1970s was called the "me" decade. To 1960s slogans such as "peace and love," this era added such classics as "I'm OK, you're OK." Jewelry got those messages across on basic buttons, inscribed on pendants, or—in fancier variations—surrounded by designs in colored enamel. Even more personal was jewelry embellished with signs of the zodiac. For the activist, there was jewelry commemorating endangered animal species: a "save the whales" button was a favorite. An American political extinction was commemorated with a Watergate gem novelty—a brooch of an elephant wearing a listening device over its ears.

In 1973 the price of gold rocketed to $120 an ounce (silver hardly de-

Shell necklace and bracelet (above) were typical of the huge size, sculptural shapes, and use of "natural" materials favored during this period (signed "Cadoro"). For both sexes: a treasury of gold-metal chains, baubles, and bangles (opposite page), and "meaningful" pendants, by Swank (opposite page, above). Body jewelry was still influential in the 1970s, with that era's own twist, such as a version done in craftsy-looking wooden beads and leather strips (opposite page).

served the designation "precious" at a mere $2.59 an ounce), playing havoc with the stock market—and with the costume jewelry business. The value of gold, coupled with the concept that "small is beautiful," conspired to reduce precious jewelry in size, and its costume imitations as well. The resulting pieces were less than spectacular: plain, skinny "gold-" look bracelets and chains that could be worn alone or dangling a single pendant (an arrow, a heart, an initial). Earrings were timid, tiny gold studs, perhaps with a single, could-be-precious colored stone in the center.

The look of gold shone throughout the 1970s, coloring jewelry and accessories. In 1977 the Metropolitan Museum of Art in New York City held a block-busting exhibition of the artifacts of King Tutankhamen. The sumptuous gold of these ancient objects, and the motifs of the objects themselves, influenced the design of both real and costume jewelry. Egyptian themes swept the land of jewelry with a force not felt since the Tutmania of the 1920s. The pharaoh, the asp, and slave and scarab bracelets were all popular items.

Gold was also the preferred color and metal for the 1970s disco doll. In 1977 New York City's famed discothèque Studio 54 opened; so did the film *Saturday Night Fever*, celebrating disco dancing. Proper attire included shiny, metallic-looking fabrics accessorized with gold (or gold-metal) chains, golden leather belts, golden platform sandals, and gold handbags.

The sinister flip side of the golden girl next door was the "tart" à la 1940s, revived by couture and theatrically made up and adorned. Her bad little sister (and brother) was the punk, who glued rainbow-colored hair into a commanche spike and painted fingernails black. A fierce subcult of the disco scene, punk's audacious style, attitude, and vociferous energy never did become a part of mainstream culture, but some of its trademarks—exaggerated hair, heavy make-up, and black leather—did. Punk jewelry was another story. The ordinary safety pin, pierced through the ear was a punk trademark, alternatively worn pinned in rows along the outer edge of the ear. Brave fashionables punctured their cheeks and nostrils with the same hardware—not a look for the squeamish. Real dog collars and leather armbands bristling with spikes, studs, grommets, and thick chains were also standard decorative equipment for punks.

In London designer Zandra Rhodes raised the lowly safety pin to the heights of elegance, adopting it as embellishment for her couture dresses. She borrowed the fabric of the punks' "altered states" too, noting, "Rips and tears are as valid ways to handle fabric as pleating is, and chains and safety pins are simply alternative, non-traditional decorations for the seventies."

The 1970s did have its own crop of artisan jewelry designers. Two pioneers, at opposite ends of the fashion pole, left their mark on costume jewelry in the late 1970s, an influence that extended well into the 1980s. In 1974 Tiffany's in New York City introduced Italian designer Elsa Peretti. Working in silver, horn, ebony, and ivory, she created tiny, streamlined "lima-bean-" and "tear-" shaped pendants on fine chains, and necklaces of "diamonds by the yard" (small cut stones spaced a few inches apart on a chain). Her spare, understated work fit the pervailing mood of the times; the beautifully sculpted pieces perfectly complimented the fashions of Halston, the ruling king of American style, whose fluid, draped clothes in luxe fabrics had elegant good manners and needed only the most minimal ornament. Peretti accessorized his collections, and she was hugely successful.

Radically different from Peretti's studied smoothness were the bold, made-by-hand pieces of designer Robert Lee Morris (who established the Artwear Gallery for jewelry in New York City). Morris worked in oxidized copper, brass, and other gold-plated metals. Every hammer dent and tap showed, and his pieces sometimes had an unsettling scale: metal necklaces draped across the body, breastplates covered most of the breast, chokers were strung with weighty, mothball-sized beads, bracelets wrapped the wrist, gladiator style. This was passionate, personal, rugged, ornament that needed a new state of mind for its wearing. Its prices were new too, on the same level as diamonds and gold jewelry. Yet, with its generous scale and use of non-precious materials, Morris's jewelry made an inverse statement of prestige.

Except for a few outbursts, and the invasion of punk, the era of the 1970s was short on thrills and chills—and humor. With a characteristic seriousness, it relished two fashion books—*Dress for Success* and *The Power Look*—enough to put them on the best-seller list. The businesslike style would continue of course, but one could look forward to the 1980s to re-introduce a little craziness.

he 1980s paired, tripled, and quadrupled almost any kind of style —and jewelry—together. Notable influences on costume jewelry included street fashion, giving rise to the popular oversized earrings and armloads of mismatched bracelets (for women and men); male pop stars (Michael Jackson, Prince); the overdressed doyennes of television soap operas such as "Dynasty" and "Dallas"; and the real glitz of Diana, Princess of Wales. The highly personal styles of ornamentation of rock stars Cyndi Lauper and Madonna trickled up into high fashion, beyond the circles of their dress-alike fans; these two ladies were also responsible for reviving "antique" costume jewelry—or jewelry that just looked like it was vintage. On the side of the classics, Chanel's costume gems, revamped by Karl Lagerfeld, continued to maintain their unique and ageless appeal. Once history has its way, however, these dazzlers may not last the reshuffle. After all, any ring could fit the fickle finger of fashion.

A pair of signal looks for the 1980s: cast-metal nameplate (above), and the classic ebullience of Chanel's costume jewelry style (opposite page).

NOTES

P. 19: "Fashion has decided that all we need ask of ornament": *Vogue*, January 15, 1927, p. 62.

P. 19: "She wears 5 million francs' worth of pearls": *Collier's*, November 12, 1927, p. 48.

P. 20: **AMERICAN JEWELERS:** "According to those dealing in the humble gems": *New York Times*, January 27, 1929, sec. 10, p. 6.

P. 20: "Most of us count a month": *The Delineator*, March 1927, p. 45.

P. 20: "The woman of uncultivated taste": Emily Post, *Etiquette* (New York: Funk & Wagnalls, 1928), p. 580.

P. 22: "The action of instruments": Arthur Pulos, *American Design Ethic* (Cambridge, Mass.: MIT Press, 1983), p. 295.

P. 22: "Simplicity is the cocktail in art.": *Style*, January 1928, p. 28.

P. 24: "Those who design jewelry today": *Jeweler's Circular*, February 23, 1928, p. 108.

P. 25: "New methods of setting jewelry": *Fashionable Dress*, October 1927, p. 21.

P. 25: "nailheads" and "Chanel stones": *Women's Wear Daily*, March 15 and February 23, 1928, n.p.

P. 25: "Modern, too": *Fashionable Dress*, October 1927, p. 46.

P. 25: "As the memory of the Great War" and "now notable by the manner": *Jeweler's Circular*, March 22, 1928, p. 47.

P. 25: "chic on the edge of poverty": Ruth Lynam, ed., *Couture* (New York: Doubleday, 1972), p. 118.

P. 25: "Modern simplicities are rich": Giulia Veronesi, *Style and Design: 1909–1929* (New York: George Braziller, 1968), p. 305.

P. 27: "Pearls are so becoming women": *The Delineator*, December 1926, p. 37.

P. 27: It was reported that her Majesty: *Jeweler's Circular*, October 27, 1926, p. 62.

P. 27: As Orienta advertised: *Jeweler's Circular*, October 27, 1926, p. 8.

P. 28: "Even the poor working girl": *Jeweler's Circular*, October 27, 1926, notes, p. 3.

P. 28: "It was hard to tell where Cartier stopped": Hans Nadelhoffer, *Cartier.* (New York: H.N. Abrams, 1984), p. 230.

P. 28: "A long string of even the most beautiful pearls": *Vogue:* August 17, 1929, p. 129.

P. 29: "A Spanish beauty who appeared": Cecil Beaton, *The Glass of Fashion* (London: Weidenfeld & Nicolson, 1954), p. 166.

P. 32: "Who says it's an old Spanish custom": *New York Times*, August 4, 1929, sec. 1, p.29.

P. 33: "Spanish topaz is 'le dernier cri' ": *Women's Wear Daily*, January 27, 1927, p. 29.

P. 33: "grotto blue jewelry": *Women's Wear Daily*, July 7, 1927, p. 2.

P. 34: "brilliant example" and "Her hunting costume": *Harper's Bazar* [sic], March 1924, p. 140.

P. 34: "they wish to be transformed into Egyptian dancing girls": quoted in Michael and Ariane Batterberry, *Mirror, Mirror: A Social History of Fashion* (New York: Holt, Rinehart & Winston, 1977), p. 274.

P. 36: "To women there is a primitive barbarism": *Vogue*, September 23, 1923, p. 56.

P. 37: "Pleating was never better": *Vogue*, April 1923, p. 41.

P. 37: "Novelty in makeup": *New York Times*, August 28, 1927, fashion page.

P. 38: "the women . . . looked as though": Liane de Pougy, *My Blue Notebooks* (New York: Harper & Row, 1980), p. 206.

P. 38: "All the ladies": quoted in Veronesi, p. 79.

P. 38: "jewels like a thug's dream of Paradise": *Harper's Bazaar*, August 1928, p. 114.

P. 38: "The dim thighs": quoted in Veronesi, p. 78.

P. 40 **SEMI-PRECIOUS STONES:** "When she wears semi-precious jewelry": *Vogue*, February 15, 1928, p. 53.

P. 40: "Very chic is a long tassel": *New York Times*, December 29, 1929, sec. 2, p. 13.

P. 43: "Barbaric jewelry shows the rush back to the natural": *Jeweler's Circular*, May 31, 1928, p. 49.

P. 44: "Bits of rough turquoise": *Jeweler's Circular*, February 17, 1926, p. 61.

P. 44: "jewelry fashions in Paris today" and "some women appear to be wearing gauntlets": *Jeweler's Circular*, June 27, 1929, p. 42.

P. 45: "Well to make sure": *Jeweler's Circular*, October 4, 1928, p. 49.

P. 46: "No color presents such a problem": *New York Times*, September 29, 1929, sec. 2, p. 15.

P. 47: "Bracelets made of cubes": *Jeweler's Circular*, August 2, 1928, p. 45.

P. 48: "Airplane earrings are worn": *Jeweler's Circular*, January 3, 1929, p. 38.

P. 49: "a little 'safety first' fetish": *Style*, January 1928, ed. note, p. 2.

P. 50: **BEACH JEWELRY:** "The spectacle of a woman wearing a white satin costume": *Jeweler's Circular*, August 2, 1928, p. 45.

P. 55: "the backwards turn of feminine fashion": *National Jeweler*, May 1930, p. 37.

P. 55: "We have come to the River of Doubt": *Pictorial Review*, winter 1931, p. 5.

P. 55: "You will see the typical New York Venus": Cecil Beaton, *Cecil Beaton's New York* (Philadelphia: J.B. Lippincott Co., 1938), p. 36.

P. 55: "Their make-up is theatrical": *Mademoiselle*, November 1937, p. 21.

P. 55: "Men . . . welcome again": *Pictorial Review*, spring 1930, p. 2.

P. 55: "Nina, Marion, and their crowd": *Junior League* magazine, January 1934, p. 10.

P. 56: "It is vulgar to be rich": quoted in *Vogue*, January 18, 1930, p. 50.

P. 56: "may well confuse a genius": *Style Arts*, spring 1936, p. 15.

P. 58: "Women are going weaker sex": *Vogue*, January 1, 1935, n.p.

P. 58: "We have our depressing responsibilities": *Junior League* magazine July 1932, p. 34.

P. 58: "Evening clothes are strangely glamorous": *Style*, October 1934, p. 7.

P. 59: "Mrs. Trefusis' party at the Tour Eiffel": *Vogue*, August 1, 1939, p. 23.

P. 59: "verged on the border of fussiness": *National Jeweler*, May 1930, p. 37.

P. 59: "The early 1900s spirit": *Women's Wear Daily*, July 7, 1933, sec. 1, p. 1.

P. 60: "need no longer squirm in her final resting place": *Style*, May 1932, p. 27.

P. 62: "Sky blue and aquamarine blue": *National Jeweler*, May 1930, p. 42.

P. 63: "scarcely more than a dusting of powder over the legs": *Pictorial Review*, fall 1930, p. 21.

P. 63: "Black, as usual": *Style*, February 1935, p. 12.

P. 67: "What completely stunned the Western world": *Vogue*, May 1935, p. 76.

P. 67: "all of the Paris couturiers": *Herald Tribune*, November 12, 1933, sec. 3, p. 7.

P. 67: "These are the dancing girl bracelets": November 14, 1933, no sec., n.p.

P. 68: "bulk and more bulk": *Vogue*, July 15, 1933, p. 20.

P. 68: "carved from a single piece of stone": *National Jeweler*, October 1930, p. 38.

P. 68: "a solid piece of composition": *National Jeweler*, May 1930, p. 38.

P. 68: "inspired seemingly by the paper frill on a hambone": *National Jeweler*, May 1930, p. 47.

P. 69: "petals, leaves, spikes": *National Jeweler*, August 1930, p. 21.

P. 69: "like hundreds of crystalline bubbles": *Dry Goods Economist*, March 1932, p. 46.

P. 70: "Don't write—telegraph mood of the present day": *Arts and Decoration*, November 1933, p. 6.

P. 70: 'Design, is affecting our daily bread': *Arts and Decoration*, November 1933, p. 6.

P. 70: "It has at last dawned on us": *American Magazine of Art*, August 1934, p. 424.

P. 72: " "mechanical splendor" and "the bolder": *Harper's Bazaar*, May 1935, p. 75.

P. 73: **CLIPS:** "Rhinestone clips": *Dress Essentials*, May 1929, p. 28.

P. 74: "By night we're brilliant": *Pictorial Review*, spring 1930, p. 25.

P. 74: "rob comment from your rival's to your hat": *New York Times*, March 17, 1939, no sec., n.p.

P. 75: **PLASTICS:** "looks massive, feels light": *Jeweler's Circular*, March 1934, p. 59 (advertisement).

P. 76: "her own particular form of ugliness" and "But then": Cecil Beaton, *Cecil Beaton's New York*, p. 36.

P. 76: "Do you want to look pretty or smart?": *Ladies' Home Journal*, March 1933, p. 29.

P. 76: "Salvador Dali": *Women's Wear Daily*, August 6, 1936, front page.

P. 77: **SCHIAPARELLI:** "Has she not the air": quoted in *Harper's Bazaar*, April 1937, p. 73.

P. 77: "Materials should either be": *Fashion Accessories*, December 1929, p. 25.

P. 77: "Belts were amusing": *National Jeweler*, October 1931, p. 47.

P. 78: "Of growing interest" and "All the romantic gaiety": *California Stylist*, June 1938, p. 32.

P. 79: "With active sports togs, Bette": *Jeweler's Circular*, July 1939, p. 17.

P. 79: "Bizarre and exciting novelty": *Dress Accessories*, March 1938, p. 22.

P. 80: **BUTTONS:** "Old costumes are reborn": *The Delineator*, December 1935, p. 29.

P. 80: **BLACKMOOR PINS:** "Have I ever shown you": Diana Vreeland, *D.V.* (New York: A.A. Knopf, 1984), p. 53.

P. 81: **MARTHA SLEEPER:** "A pretty and remarkable young lady": *Collier's*, December 1938, p. 20.

P. 83: "War changes a lot of things": *Fashion Accessories*, September 1942, p. 63.

P. 83: "The woman in overalls": *Mademoiselle*, October 1942, p. 65.

P. 83: "I often wear trousers": *Fashion Digest*, spring 1940. p. 35.

P. 84: "Are we mice" and "resourcefulness and inventiveness": *Fashion Digest*, fall 1940. p. 29.

P. 84: "She'll have loyalties": *Mademoiselle*, March 1941, p. 103.

P. 84: "A lapel pin": *Charm*, May 1944, p. 35.

P. 85: "Costume jewelry, strange": *Jeweler's Circular*, November 1942, p. 77.

P. 85: "What is the last word" and "Wood. Colored plastics": *New York Times Magazine*, September 13, 1942, p. 42.

P. 86: "She wore a steel-gray": *The Lady in the Lake*, in *The Raymond Chandler Omnibus*, (New York: A. A. Knopf, 1969), p. 473.

P. 87: "Jewelry goes so far" and "It may be a metal belt": *Fashion Accessories*, June 1946, p. 39.

P. 87: "To see what the trend is": *Collier's*, December 15, 1945, p. 93.

P. 88: "The costume jewelry industry": *Fashion Accessories*, January 1941, p. 7.

P. 88: "aroused much interest among Chicagoans": *Fashion Accessories*, May 1944, p. 23.

P. 90: "quite durable and dyed in many colors": *Women's Wear Daily*, January 19, 1941, p. 21.

P. 90: "Jewelry firms are taking up": *Women's Wear Daily*, February 5, 1943, p. 23.

P. 91: "A novelty is a big football pin": *Women's Wear Daily*, August 8, 1941, p. 21.

P. 93: "No more does the picture of Brenda Frazier": *California Stylist*, February 1943, p. 44.

P. 97: "Bare, beautiful Indian jewelry" and "Many costumes": *Fashion Digest*, winter 1939–40, p. 21.

P. 97: "Any frou-frou": *Vogue*, September 1946, p. 126.

P. 98: "In this 24 hours-a-day": *California Stylist*, February 1943, p. 57.

P. 98: "Last year's hat": *Smart*, February 1941, p. 31.

P. 98: "*Gone With the Wind*": *New York Times Magazine*, January 7, 1940, p. 8.

P. 99: "interesting style points": *Smart*, February 1941, p. 30.

P. 103: "smaller and more finely wrought": *Jeweler's Circular*, December 1941, p. 37.

P. 104: "The arts and crafts of the Indian": *Women's Wear Daily*, January 3, 1941, p. 21.

P. 104: "All our important American stylists": *Fashion Accessories*, March 1941, p. 8.

P. 104: "They wanted jewelry made in Mexico": *Women's Wear Daily*. August 13, 1943, p. 18.

P. 127: "They are settling down": *Harper's Bazaar*, February 1957, p. 104.

P. 127: "Mrs. A": *Vogue*, October 15, 1954, p. 85.

P. 128 **BIG RINGS**: "Evenings at home": *Women's Wear Daily*, August 3, 1951, p. 13.

P. 128: "dinner suits and coats": *Vogue*, October 1, 1954, p. 102.

P. 128: "evenings of Canasta": *Flair*, October 1950, p. 51.

P. 129: "It was a timid woman": *New York Times*, January 1, 1960, sec. 4, p. 36.

P. 129: "misty slate, deep charcoal": *Harper's Bazaar*, September 1959, p. 168.

P. 130: "the fashionable way" and "through caftan coats": *New York Times Magazine*, October 30, 1955, p. 54.

P. 132: "Counterbalancing the sharp, pure line" and "happening all around you": *Harper's Bazaar*, March 1955, p. 113.

P. 135: "Yves St. Laurent at Dior": *Harper's Bazaar*, September 1959, p. 168.

P. 136: "To go with the stylishly casual": *Life*, November 24, 1957, p. 75.

P. 138: "Too much jewelry": *Life*, November 24, 1957, p. 75.

P. 138: "Golden opportunities": *Vogue*, March 1954, p. 122.

P. 140: "Both the farm lady and the First Lady": *Jeweler's Circular*, July 1956, p. 38.

P. 141: "Because all eyes": *New York Times*, January 20, 1953, sec. 4, p. 28.

P. 141: "Pills to keep you going": *Harper's Bazaar*, July 1959, special section, p. 1.

P. 145: "The Old Guard": *Women's Wear Daily*, July 19, 1965, p. 1.

P. 145: "Nobody ever looked like them": *Vogue*, November 15, 1965, p. 122.

P. 145: The new leg": quoted in Marilyn Bender, *The Beautiful People* (New York: Coward-McCann, 1967), p. 84.

P. 145: "One of our national concerns": *Ladies' Home Journal*, July 1962, p. 56.

P. 146: "zip up, pop on, and just go": *Vogue*, November 19, 1965, p. 123.

P. 146: "Fashion has ceased": Ruth Lynam, ed., *Couture: An Illustrated History of the Great Paris Designers and their Creations* (New York: Doubleday, 1972), p. 235.

P. 146: "There was a time when clothes": *Vogue*, August 1966, p. 86.

P. 147: "the simplicity of fashion-editor taste": Bender, p. 49.

P. 147: "Sonny's lionheart haircut": *Vogue*, December 1965, p.28.

P. 147: "Every era has its favorite capital": David Baily and Peter Evans, *Goodbye Baby & Amen: A Saraband for the Sixties* (New York: Coward-McCann, 1969), p. 164.

P. 149: "Over the shoulder, a load": *Vogue*, September 15, 1965, p. 81.

P. 151: **BODY JEWELRY**: "This way every woman": *Woman's Wear Daily*, August 1, 1969, p. 16.

P. 151: **BODY JEWELRY**: "meant for young, modest-sized bosoms": *New York Times*, February 12, 1969, no sec., p. 42.

P. 153: "Surely few Americans": *New York Times*, September 24, 1967, no sec., p.25.

P. 153: **MEN'S JEWELRY**: "The hippie clanking around": *New York Times*, March 29, 1968, no sec., p. 44.

P. 153: **MEN'S JEWELRY**: "If we know a man": *New York Times*, March 29, 1968, no sec., p. 44.

P. 153: **MEN'S JEWELRY**: "I don't think beads are effeminate": *Newsweek*, April 1, 1968, p. 99.

P. 155: "The patterned fur coat": *Harper's Bazaar*, December 1967, p. 125.

P. 157: "brisk, bizarre young women": Lynam, p. 201.

P. 157: "aluminum necklaces-cum-bras": Lynam, p. 212.

P. 157: "The space-age love of geometric forms": *Jeweler's Circular*, June 1966, p. 38.

P. 158: "A lot of jingling brass hardware": *Harper's Bazaar*, December 1967, p. 125.

P. 159: "In the Age of Aquarius": *New York Times*, November 28, 1969, no sec., p. 45.

P. 159: ' People are wearing crosses": *New York Times*, November 28, 1969, no sec., p. 45.

P. 159: "the square brooch looks medieval": *Women's Wear Daily*, August 13, 1965, p. 13.

P. 160: "fashion cannot come up from the street": *New York Times Magazine*, February 14, 1967, p. 46.

P. 162: **KENNETH JAY LANE**: "ladies from the Social Register": *Saturday Evening Post*, September 7, 1968, p. 40.

P. 162: **KENNETH JAY LANE**: "On any given day": *Saturday Evening Post*, September 7, 1968, p. 40.

P. 163: **WIGGED-OUT HAIR**: "a splendor of hair": *Vogue*, November 1, 1966, p. 194.

P. 165: "It became chic to cut back": *Time*, April 4, 1977, p. 65.

Pp. 165 "It's so chic not to look moneyed": *Women's Wear Daily*, March 4, 1971, p. 12.
–66:

P. 168: "Rips and tears are as valid ways": *Vogue*, September 1977, p. 181.

PHOTOGRAPH CREDITS

L: Left   R: Right   C: Center   T: Top   B: Bottom

Front cover: photograph by Max Vadukul; make-up by Linda Mason; hair by René Gelston; stylist, Ana Roth; model, Shelley Boyd. (Jewelry courtesy of Jules van Rouge)

Back cover: photograph by Cecil Beaton (Courtesy of Sotheby's, London)

Front flap: photograph by Max Vadukul; make-up by Sonia Kashuk; hair by René Gelston; stylist, Jody Shields; model, Shelley Boyd. (Jewelry courtesy of Jules van Rouge)

Back flap: photograph by Max Vadukul; make-up by Linda Mason; hair by Stephen Price; stylist, Catherine Laroche; model, Maripol. (Jewelry courtesy of Maripol)

P. 1: photograph by Max Vadukul; model, Ruby Andrade. (Location and vintage jewelry courtesy of Norman Crider Antiques, Trump Tower, New York City)

Pp. 2–3: photograph by Max Vadukul; make-up by Linda Mason; hair by René Gelston; stylist, Jody Shields; model, Lucy Cunningham. (Jewelry and Balenciaga sweater courtesy of Mark Walsh)

Pp. 4–5: photograph by Max Vadukul; make-up by Linda Mason with Diane Mentken; hair by Eric Gonzalez for Oribe at Parachute; stylist, Ana Roth; sweaters by Lyle & Scott; scarf hat by Mary Bright; models (from left to right), Cathy Carapella, Mary Bright, Patsy Abbott, Debra Dale McCown, Brian Watson, Ann Shakeshaft, Cindy Shulga.

Pp. 6–7: photograph by Max Vadukul; make-up by Sonia Kashuk; hair by Eric Gonzalez for Oribe at Parachute; stylist, Ana Roth; model, Eugenie Vincent. (Jewelry courtesy of Mark Walsh)

P. 8: photograph by Max Vadukul; make-up by Sonia Kashuk; hair by René Gelston; stylist, Jody Shields; model, Eugenia Bartels. (Jewelry courtesy of Napier)

Pp. 10–11: photograph by Max Vadukul; make-up by Linda Mason; hair by René Gelston; stylist, Ana Roth; model, Linda Mason.

P. 13: photograph by Max Vadukul; make-up by Linda Mason; hair by René Gelston; stylist, Catherine Laroche; model, Alison Houtte. (Jewelry courtesy of Wendy Gell)

P. 14: photograph by Max Vadukul; make-up by Linda Mason; hair by René Gelston; stylist, Ana Roth; model, Lucy Cunningham. (Jewelry courtesy of Barneys, New York City)

P. 16: photograph by Max Vadukul; make-up by Linda Mason; hair by René Gelston; stylist, Catherine Laroche; model, Rebecca Wright.

P. 18T: photograph by Henri Jacques Lartigue. (Courtesy of Christie's, New York City)

Pp. 18–19: illustrations copyright © 1927, The Hearst Corportion. (Courtesy of *Harper's Bazaar*)

P. 21: *Madame Bijoux*, photograph by Brassai. (Courtesy of Christie's, New York City)

P. 22B: courtesy of Stein & Ellbogen, Chicago.

P. 23: photograph by Max Vadukul; make-up by Linda Mason; dress by Angel Estrada; stylist, Ana Roth; model, Vivian Horan. (Jewelry by Les Bernard)

P. 25T: courtesy of Chanel.

P. 26: photograph by Max Vadukul; make-up by Linda Mason; hair by René Gelston; stylist, Ana Roth; model, Meg Grosswendt. (Jewelry courtesy of Marvella)

P. 28: photograph by Baron De Meyer. (Courtesy of Christie's, New York City)

P. 30T: photograph by Paul Outerbridge. (Courtesy of Christie's, New York City)

P. 31TL: photograph courtesy of Napier.

P. 32C: necklace courtesy of Susan Freeman.

P. 33: necklace courtesy of Napier.

P. 34: necklace courtesy of Tamara Schneider.

P. 35: bracelet courtesy of Lizi Boyd.

P. 36L: illustration courtesy of Napier.

P. 36R: photograph by Max Vadukul.

P. 38C: illustration copyright © 1923, The Hearst Corporation. (Courtesy of *Harper's Bazaar*)

P. 39C: necklace and bracelet courtesy of Virginia Fuentes.

P. 39R: bracelet courtesy of Mark Walsh.

P. 40T: necklace courtesy of Tamara Schneider.

P. 42: photograph by Cecil Beaton. (Courtesy of Sotheby's, London)

P. 48B: courtesy of Coro.

P. 49B: ring courtesy of Susan Freeman.

P. 51TL, BR: shoes and handbag courtesy of Mark Walsh.

P. 51C: illustration courtesy of the *National Jeweler*.

P. 51BL: illustration courtesy of Napier.

P. 54: photograph by Max Vadukul; make-up by Linda Mason; stylist, Ana Roth; model, Marilyn Cooperman.

P. 55B: brooch courtesy of Mark Walsh.

P. 56: photographs copyright © 1939, The Hearst Corporation. (*Courtesy of Harper's Bazaar*)

P. 57: bracelet courtesy of Mark Walsh.

P. 58T: photograph copyright © 1939 The Hearst Corporation. (Courtesy of *Harper's Bazaar*)

Pp. 58–59C: bracelets courtesy of Susan Freeman.

P. 59C: photograph by Toni Frissel. (Courtesy of Bergdorf Goodman)

P. 60T: brooches courtesy of Mark Walsh.

P. 60C: photograph by Max Vadukul. (Bracelet courtesy of Mrs. Gerald Rosenberger)

P. 61R: earrings courtesy of Norman Crider Antiques, Trump Tower, New York City.

P. 64: photograph by Horst. (Courtesy of Horst)

P. 65: photographs copyright © 1939 The Hearst Corporation. (Courtesy of *Harper's Bazaar*)

P. 66T: photograph by Hoyningen-Huene, copyright © 1939 The Hearst Corporation. (Courtesy of *Harper's Bazaar*)

P. 66B: illustration courtesy of Napier.

P. 68B: bracelet courtesy of Susan Freeman.

P. 69T: necklace courtesy of Sanford Moss of Miriam Haskell.

P. 70TR: bracelet courtesy of Mark Walsh.

P. 71B: illustration courtesy of Napier.

P. 72: jewelry courtesy of Catherine Laroche.

P. 73: photograph courtesy of Napier.

P. 74B: brooch courtesy of Susan Freeman.

P. 75L: photograph by Max Vadukul; make-up by Stephen Price; model, Susan Freeman. (Jewelry courtesy of Susan Freeman)

P. 76: necklace photograph courtesy of The Brooklyn Museum.

P. 77T: photograph by Cecil Beaton. (Courtesy of Sotheby's, London)

P. 77B: brooch courtesy of Mark Walsh.

P. 78: necklaces courtesy of Susan Freeman.

P. 79T: necklace courtesy of Sheila Parkert.

P. 79B: necklace courtesy of Susan Freeman.

P. 80L: brooches courtesy of Mrs. Gerald Rosenberger.

P. 80TR: blackamoor pins courtesy of Norman Crider Antiques, Trump Tower, New York City.

P. 81BC, BR: illustrations courtesy of *Harper's & Queen*.

P. 82: photograph by Max Vadukul; make-up by Linda Mason; hair by Gerard Bollei; model, Linda Mason. (Jewelry courtesy of Ilene Chazanof, New York City)

P. 83: brooch courtesy of The Antique Arcade, Glens Falls, New York.

P. 84T: photograph courtesy of Arpad Necessories.

P. 88T: brooch courtesy of Leslie Chin.

P. 89: photograph by Max Vadukul; stylist, Catherine Laroche; model, Helmut Krone.

Pp. 90B, 91T: photographs courtesy of Joanne Moonon.

P. 92: photograph courtesy of Trifari.

P. 93T: brooch courtesy of The Antique Arcade, Glens Falls, New York.

P. 93B: brooch courtesy of Mrs. Gerald Rosenberger.

P. 95: photograph by Max Vadukul; model, John Sahag.

P. 97: photograph by Louise Dahl-Wolfe. (Courtesy of Staley Wise Gallery, New York City)

P. 101: photograph by Max Vadukul; make-up by Sonia Kashuk; hair by Eric Gonzalez for Oribe at Parachute; stylist and model, Ana Roth. (Jewelry courtesy of Ilene Chazanof, New York City)

P. 102: photograph by Max Vadukul; hair by René Gelston; stylist, Ana Roth; model, Damaris Webb.

Pp. 103–105: jewelry courtesy of Kate Loy.

P. 106TL: buttons courtesy of Betty Earland.

P. 106TC: Jacques Fath necklace courtesy of Mark Walsh.

P. 106BL: photograph courtesy of Arpad Necessories.

P. 107T: photographs of the Duchess of Windsor's jewelry courtesy of Sotheby's Inc. © 1986.

P. 107C: brooch courtesy of Douglas Stanley.

P. 107BL: pin courtesy of Virginia Fuentes.

P. 107BR: earrings courtesy of Norman Crider Antiques, Trump Tower, New York City.

Color section, photographs pages 109–124 by Max Vadukul

P. 109: make-up by Linda Mason; stylist, Jody Shields; model, Honey Aldrich. (Miriam Haskell jewelry courtesy of Norman Crider Antiques, Trump Tower, New York City, and Barneys, New York City; watch courtesy of the author)

P. 110: make-up by Sonia Kashuk; hair by René Gelston; stylist, Jody Shields; model, Shelley Boyd. (Jewelry courtesy of Jules van Rouge)

P. 111: make-up by Linda Mason; hat sculpture by René Gelston; Astroturf jacket by Carl Wolf; stylist, Ana Roth; model, Ariane Koizumi.

P. 112: make-up by Linda Mason; stylist, Ana Roth; model, Susan Sultan. (Jewelry courtesy of Melmar Plastics)

P. 113: jewelry courtesy of Sanford G. Moss, available at Barneys, New York City.

P. 114: make-up by Linda Mason; hair by René Gelston; skirt by Williwear; stylist, Catherine Laroche; model, Alison Houtte. (Jewelry courtesy of Wendy Gell)

P. 115: make-up by Linda Mason; stylist, Jody Shields; model, Marina Nixon. (Jewelry courtesy of Norman Crider Antiques, Trump Tower, New York City)

Pp. 116–117: jewelry courtesy of Mark Walsh.

P. 118: make-up and hair by Diane Mentken; stylist, Jody Shields; model, Karen Binns. (Jewelry courtesy of Barney's, New York City)

P. 119: make-up by Sonya Kashuk; hair by René Gelston; stylist, Ana Roth; model, Cindy Crawford. (Jewelry courtesy of Jacques Libuono)

P. 120: make-up by Linda Mason; stylist, Ana Roth. (Jewelry courtesy of Trifari)

P. 121: make-up by Linda Mason; hair by René Gelston; stylist, Catherine Laroche; model, Meg Grosswendt. (Jewelry courtesy of Marvella)

Pp. 122–123: make-up by Sonya Kashuk; hair by Eric Gonzalez for Oribe at Parachute; stylist, Ana Roth; model, Eugenie Vincent. (Jewelry courtesy of Mark Walsh)

P. 124: jewelry courtesy of Cadoro.

P. 126: photograph by Max Vadukul; stylist, Jody Shields; model, Susan Batchelder. (Necklace courtesy of Norman Crider Antiques, Trump Tower, New York City; earrings courtesy of Napier)

P. 127C: necklace courtesy of Tina Chow.

P. 127B: photographs courtesy of The Fashion Group.

Pp. 128–129: photographs courtesy of Napier.

P. 130T: photograph courtesy of The Fashion Group.

P. 130C: photograph courtesy of Napier.

P. 131: necklace courtesy of Norman Crider Antiques, Trump Tower, New York City.

P. 132: brooch and earrings courtesy of Trifari.

P. 133C: photograph courtesy of the National Portrait Gallery, London.

P. 133BL: brooch courtesy of Trifari.

P. 133BR: brooch cortesy of Mark Walsh.

P. 134T: brooch courtesy of Mark Walsh.

P. 134C: photograph by Lousie Dahl-Wolfe. (Courtesy of Staley Wise Gallery, New York City)

P. 135: photographs courtesy of The Fashion Group.

P. 136: necklace courtesy of Monet.

P. 137: photograph by Max Vadukul; make-up by Linda Mason; stylist, Catherine Laroche; model, Thea Derecola. (Jewelry courtesy of Napier)

P. 138: brooch courtesy of Napier.

P. 139C: photograph courtesy of Trifari.

P. 140B: brooch courtesy of Virginia Fuentes.

P. 141: bracelet courtesy of Napier; brooches courtesy of Trifari.

P. 142: brooch and jewelry box courtesy of Mark Walsh.

P. 142TC: Mamie Eisenhower jewelry photograph courtesy of Trifari.

P. 143T: belts illustration courtesy of Saks Fifth Avenue.

P. 143BL: "Ike" bracelet courtesy of Susan Freeman.

P. 143BC: accessories photograph courtesy of Saks Fifth Avenue.

P. 143C: photograph courtesy of Napier.

P. 144: photograph by Max Vadukul; make-up by Sonia Kashuk; hair by René Gelston; dress courtesy of Dianne B., New York City;
stylist, Jody Shields; model, Shelley Boyd. (Jewelry courtesy of Jules van Rouge)

P. 145: bracelet courtesy of Jacques Libuono.

P. 146: photograph by Melvin Solosky; copyright © 1961 The Hearst Corporation. (Courtesy of *Harper's Bazaar*)

P. 147T (split photograph): photograph (left) courtesy of Napier; photograph (right) courtesy of Cadoro.

P. 147B: earrings courtesy of Monet.

P. 148: bracelet (center) courtesy of Bill Smith; earring and bracelet (top, bottom) courtesy of Arpad Necessories; necklace (background) courtesy of Jane Marshall.

P. 149: photograph by Gleb Derujinsky; copyright © 1962 The Hearst Corporation. (Courtesy of *Harper's Bazaar*)

P. 149 inset: photograph courtesy of Jules van Rouge.

P. 150TC: necklace courtesy of Bill Smith.

P. 150B: photograph courtesy of Kenneth Jay Lane.

P. 151L, C: photographs courtesy of Lee Menichetti.

P. 151BR: photograph courtesy of Jules van Rouge.

P. 152: photograph by Max Vadukul; stylist Jody Shields; model, Max Pinnell. (Jewelry courtesy of Monet.)

P. 154: bracelet courtesy of Susan Freeman.

P. 155: photograph by Max Vadukul; make-up

by Linda Mason; hair by René Gelston; dress by Williwear; stylist, Catherine Laroche; model, Gwen Hoyt. (Jewelry courtesy of Jacques Libuono)

P. 156: bracelet courtesy of Napier.

P. 156T: brooch courtesy of Trifari.

P. 157T: photograph courtesy of Cadoro.

P. 157C: photograph by Skrebneski. (Courtesy of Estée Lauder)

P. 157B: photograph by Bill Silano; copyright © The Hearst Corporation. (Courtesy of *Harper's Bazaar*)

P. 157R (background): jewelry courtesy of Bill Smith.

P. 158B: photograph courtesy of Kenneth Jay Lane.

P. 158 (background): jewelry courtesy of Bill Smith.

P. 159: jewelry courtesy of Trifari.

P. 159 (inset): jewelry courtesy of Mark Walsh.

P. 160 (background): photograph courtesy of Napier.

P. 160T (inset): photograph by Ryszard Horowitz; copyright © 1968 The Hearst Corporation. (Courtesy of *Harper's Bazaar*)

P. 160B (inset): photograph by James Moore; copyright © 1964 The Hearst Corporation. (Courtesy of *Harper's Bazaar*)

P. 161: photograph by Ryszard Horowitz; copyright © 1968 The Hearst Corporation. (Courtesy of *Harper's Bazaar*)

P. 161L: photograph courtesy of Yves St. Laurent.

P. 161R: jewelry courtesy of Jacques Libuono.

P. 162T: photograph by Alberto Rizzo; copyright © 1969 The Hearst Corporation. (Courtesy of *Harper's Bazaar*)

P. 162BL: photograph courtesy of Bill Smith.

P. 162C: photograph of the Duchess of Windsor's jewelry courtesy of Sotheby's, New York.

P. 163TC: photograph courtesy Jules van Rouge.

P. 163BL: illustration courtesy of Cadoro.

P. 163BR: photograph by Bill King; copyright © 1971 The Hearst Corporation (Courtesy of Harper's Bazaar)

P. 164: photograph by Max Vadukul; stylist, Jody Shields; models, Max Vadukul and Lou Salvatori. (Jewelry courtesy of Butterfly Boutique, New York City)

P. 165: jewelry courtesy of Robert Lee Morris.

P. 166T: jewelry courtesy of Napier.

P. 166C: photograph courtesy of Cadoro.

P. 167: photograph by Max Vadukul; model, Nick Lewin. (Jewelry courtesy of Napier)

P. 168: photograph courtesy of Cadoro.

P. 169TR: photograph courtesy of Swank.

P. 169B: photograph courtesy of Cadoro.

P. 170: photograph by Max Vadukul; make-up by Linda Mason; stylist, Ana Roth; model, Holly Brubach.

P. 171: photograph by Max Vadukul; stylist, Catherine Laroche; model, Ezel.

Color section, pages 177–191. Photographs by Paul Lachenauer. Art director for photographs, Jody Shields.

P. 177: Indian brooches, cup and saucer courtesy of Susan Freeman; doll and swan brooch courtesy of Catherine Laroche.

P. 178: jewelry courtesy of Norman Crider Antiques, Trump Tower, New York City.

P. 179: jewelry courtesy of Jeanne M. Golly. (Photograph reprinted courtesy of *Vogue Bellezia*)

P. 183: tablecloth courtesy of Sheila Parkert and Gregg Siefker; cake by Susan Batchelder. (Jewelry courtesy of Susan Freeman)

P. 184: Patou, Chanel, and Fath jewelry courtesy of Mark Walsh; Trifari brooch courtesy of Trifari.

P. 185: jewelry courtesy of The Antique Arcade, Glens Falls, New York, and Sheila Parkert.

P. 186: jewelry courtesy of Mark Walsh.

P. 187: jewelry courtesy of Susan Freeman.

P. 188: jewelry courtesy of Susan Freeman.

P. 189: jewelry courtesy of Mark Walsh.

P. 190: jewelry courtesy of Norman Crider Antiques, Trump Tower, New York City.

P. 191: jewelry courtesy of Jacques Libuono.

ACKNOWLEDGMENTS

It gives me great pleasure to acknowledge those who have helped with this book and to whom I have run up innumerable debts of gratitude. I'd like to thank Allison Leopold, whose encouragement, example, and critiques of the text were invaluable. Linda Mason, Catherine Laroche, and Susan Batchelder deserve special awards for their humor, patience, support, and the creative inspiration that was their gift to this volume. I am also grateful to Ann Shakeshaft and Sheila Parkert for their enthusiasm and steady guidance.

I remain indebted to Max Vadukul, whose series of portraits make up the backbone of this book. His humor, creativity, and photographic vision added to the realization of this project. Let me express my appreciation to Paul Lachenauer. His still-life photography transported jewelry into a unique and wonderful realm, and I thank him for his courtesy and exacting professionalism. Both photographers labored heroically.

I'd like to express gratitude to my editor at Rizzoli, Stephanie Salomon. She has been infinitely generous with her support and patience. Her dedication, insights, and suggestions were an enormous aid in directing the book.

Philip Zimmerman and the late Keith Davis deserve profound praise for their design of this book; they achieved singular results with what was a very complicated task.

Of the mentors and friends who were generous with their help, I'd like to thank especially Bob Gold. Tamara Schneider, Marilyn Cooperman, Susan Gosin, and Richard Barrett were constant angels; Bernard Lennon has my particular gratitude for his help. Ann Lacombe, Floyd Byars, and Lesa Salvani were wonderfully supportive.

Kindest thanks to the book's creative team: Linda Mason and Sonia Kashuk, assisted by Diane Mentken, for their glorious makeup; Ana Roth and Catherine Laroche for the perfection of their styling; and René Gelston, Eric Gonzalez, Gerard Bollei, and Stephen Price for their artful hairstyling. Thanks also to Carl Wolf for his creative costuming.

I'm indebted to Susan Freeman: her expertise, insight, and appreciation for costume jewelry were priceless. Mark Walsh deserves special gratitude for his enthusiasm and for sharing his knowledge of jewelry. Both individuals were unfailingly gracious in making their costume jewelry collections available. Cindy Shulga of Napier, Jacques Libuono, Jules van Rouge, Norman Crider, and Sanford Moss of Miriam Haskell, also have my thanks.

The models for the book had stoic patience and humor; unfortunately, lack of space didn't permit the inclusion of all their portraits. I'd like to acknowledge: Patsy Abbott, Honey Aldrich, Ruby Andrade, Christophe Ascher, John Badum, Eugenia Bartels, Felicitas Beh, Karen Binns, Shelley Boyd, Mary Bright, Wayne and Natasha Brown, Holly Brubach, Baby Bryan, Marla Buck, Sandra Canning, Cathy Carapella, Martin Cooke, Cindy Crawford, Lucy Cunningham, Debora Dale, Thea Derecola, Ezel, Stuart Freeman, Susan Freeman, Henny Garfinkel, René Gelston, Isabella Ginanneschi, Susan Gosin, Sheila Gray, Meg Grosswendt, Vivian Horan, Gwen Heyt, Alison Houtte, Ariane Koizumi, Helmut Krone, Catherine Laroche, Nick Lewin, Maripol, Linda Mason, Marina Nixon, Florence Pearse, Maylen Pierce, Max Pinnell, Courtney Regan, Ana Roth, John Sahag, Louis Salvatori, Liz Samolyk, Ann Shakeshaft, Cynthia Shulga, Susan Sultan, Lina Varquez, Eugenie Vincent, Mark Walsh, Brian Watson, Damaris Webb, and Rebecca Wright.

I am infinitely appreciative of the generosity of *Harper's Bazaar* in permitting reprints of notable photographs and illustrations: thanks to Anthony Mazzola, Betty Klarnet, and her assistant, Melissa Bedolis. Special appreciation also goes to the staff of Sotheby's and Christie's in New York and London. Thanks to Valerie Vlasaty, Dana Hawkes, Barbara Klein, Amy Murphy, and Mish Tworkowski at Sotheby's in New York, and Lydia Cullen and Nicola Redwing in London. At Christie's in New York, thanks to Claudia Gropper.

I'm obliged to the following people who helped answer requests for photographs and information: Taki Wise of the Staley Wise Gallery, New York City; Lenore Benson and Barbara Blair Randall of The Fashion Group; Susanna van Langenberg of *Harper's & Queen*; Gerry Hansen of the Jewelry Industry Council; Marina Malazasi and Sherry Winston of Condé Nast; Nancy Long of Tobé, Lee Menichetti; Steve Brody of Cadoro; Amy L. Katz and George W. Feld of Revlon; James Arpad of Arpad Necessories; Joanne Moonan; Emmett D. Chisum of the University of Wyoming; and Phyllis Melhado of Estée Lauder.

A special thank you to those who generously consented to be interviewed about costume jewelry's history: Hugh Allen, Kitty d'Alessio, James and Steven Arpad, Linda Barello, Les Bernard, Sandra Boucher, Steven Brody, Charles Buckley, John Carpaco, Tina Chow, Beth Cohen, Blanche Davinger, Genevieve Mitchell Dawson, Dick Frankovich, Arthur Freirich, Bill and Charles Ellbogen, Carl Eisenberg, John Eisenberg, Carlton Fishel, Jack Gilbert, Julius Goldman, Sarah Gowell, Irving Green, Pat Hill, Don Hobé, Martha Jackson, Claire Kelam, Max Kittay, Robert Koch, Louis Krussman, Kenneth Jay Lane, Tricia Lee, Joe Leonard, Irving Levy, Norman Lowenstein, Kate Loy, Arthur Maier, Louis Maresca, Joanne Moonan, Sanford Moss, Jean de Moüy, John Omaggio, Armand Panetta, Sig Praeger, Victor Primavera, William Rand, Mrs. Gerald Rosenberger, Carmine Russo, Bill Smith, Sol Smith, Fred Standish, Esther Tortolani, Richard Weinreich, Paulette Weisenfeld, and Helen Zannini.

For aiding the book at various stages, I'd like to express my appreciation to the following: Isabella Ginanneschi and Ann Shakeshaft for their input on the book design; Lauren Shakely and Sarah Burns at Rizzoli; my agent, Deborah Geltman, who guided the project through turbulent periods; Kathleen Sharts, Catherine Laroche, and Cathy Carapella for their research help; Shari Mayln, Vernon Jolly, Lois Joy Johnson, and Charlie Griffin for their assistance; and Susan Miller for her patient photography. I'm obliged to Photo Productions Studio in New York; our portrait sessions there were eased by the solicitous attentions of Emily Daily, Maxine Myrie, Joanne Slicker, and Kim Tylec. Special thanks also to Schnoodle Studio and Lou Salvatori in New York, who kindly allowed us to use their space for photography.

Finally, I'd like to thank my parents, Leo and Edna Shields, who encouraged me at every point along the way.

Page 177: novelties from the 1940s—hand-painted and hand-carved 3-D wooden brooches, including a swan, a horse head, a South American doll, and a pair of Indians, each measuring two inches high. Page 178: hand-set stones in breath-taking colors distinguish these brooches and clips from the 1930s-40s, signed "Eisenberg" and "Sterling." Page 179: shower of Karl Lagerfeld's witty faucet jewelry from the 1980s made of plastic, pearls, cut stones, and a metal hose (from left to right—earring, necklace, and brooch). Page 181: sinister, slightly Surrealistic pair of enameled metal pen-nib clips from the 1930s. Page 183: jolly jewelry waits for the party to start—plastic brooches with jointed limbs, each measuring up to five inches high, from the 1930-40s. Page 184: pair of intricately enameled "painted lady" clips used to grace lapels in the early 1940s, signed "Nettie Rosenstein." Page 185: game time—a winning combination of plastic and Bakelite rings (hand-carved, and hand-painted, in some cases) from the 1930s-40s (plastic crib toy figures are similar to brooches made at the same time). Page 186: dolled-up vegetables show off couturier jewelry—glass flower brooch, signed "Chanel," from the 1960s (worn by carrot); glass earrings and brooch set, signed "Jean Patou," from the 1960s (worn by potato); glass brooch, signed "Chanel," from the 1960s (worn by turnip); bird brooches, signed "Chanel," from the 1930s (worn by green pepper); rhinestone flower brooch, signed "Trifari," from the 1950s (foreground), pearl and green-glass necklace attributed to Jacques Fath, unsigned (background). Page 187: associated with California, whimsical jewelry of shells, seeds, cork, coral, wood, and nuts was worn in the 1930s and 1940s. Page 188: Hand-carved plastic bracelets, set with rhinestones and metal decorative elements, from the 1930s-40s (transparent polka-dot, fish, and flower bracelets are carved and painted on the reverse side). Page 189: mega-sized red stone necklace, signed "Dior," made in the 1950s. Page 190: enameled brooch from the 1930s depicts head of Josephine Baker, complete with a flamboyant costume headdress. Page 191: trio of enormous bracelets from the 1960s with hand-set stones, by Jacques Libuono. Endpaper: pair of showgirls costumed as pendant earrings for a 1923 Broadway dance review.

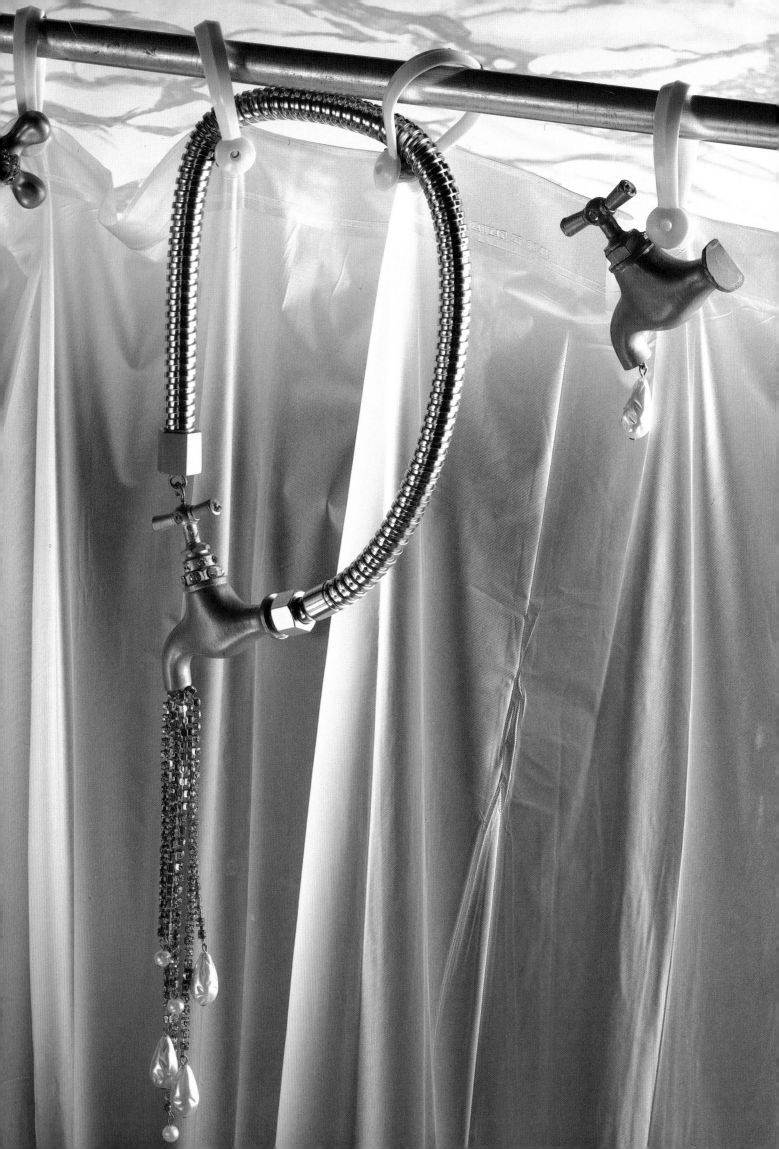

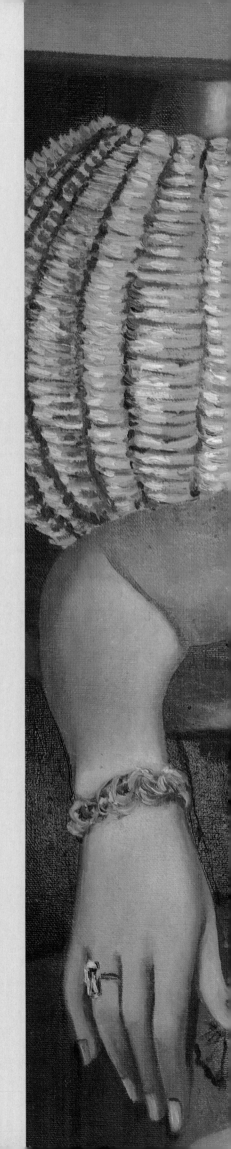

Jacket design by AGWA Productions

Also published by Rizzoli, New York:

Fashion and Surrealism
Richard Martin

American Jewelry
Glamour and Tradition
Penny Proddow and Debra Healy
Photographs by David Behl
Foreword by Ralph Esmerian

Street Style
British Design in the 80s
Catherine McDermott

Jewelry by Architects
Barbara Radice

Van Cleef & Arpels
Sylvie Raulet

Elsa Schiaparelli
Foreword by Yves Saint Laurent
Palmer White

Poiret
Yvonne Deslandres
Photographs by Jean-Michel Tardy
and Jacques Boulay

Rizzoli International Publications, Inc.
597 Fifth Avenue
New York, NY 10017